THE
MAP
DESIGN
TOOLBOX

TIME-SAVING TEMPLATES
FOR GRAPHIC DESIGN

FOR YOU

INDEX

CONTENT:

CONTINENTS
COUNTRIES
CITIES & REGIONS
TIME ZONES
CLIMATE ZONES
CURRENTS
MAGNETIC DECLINATION
VINTAGE

WORLD MAPS

NORTH AMERICA

SOUTH AMERICA

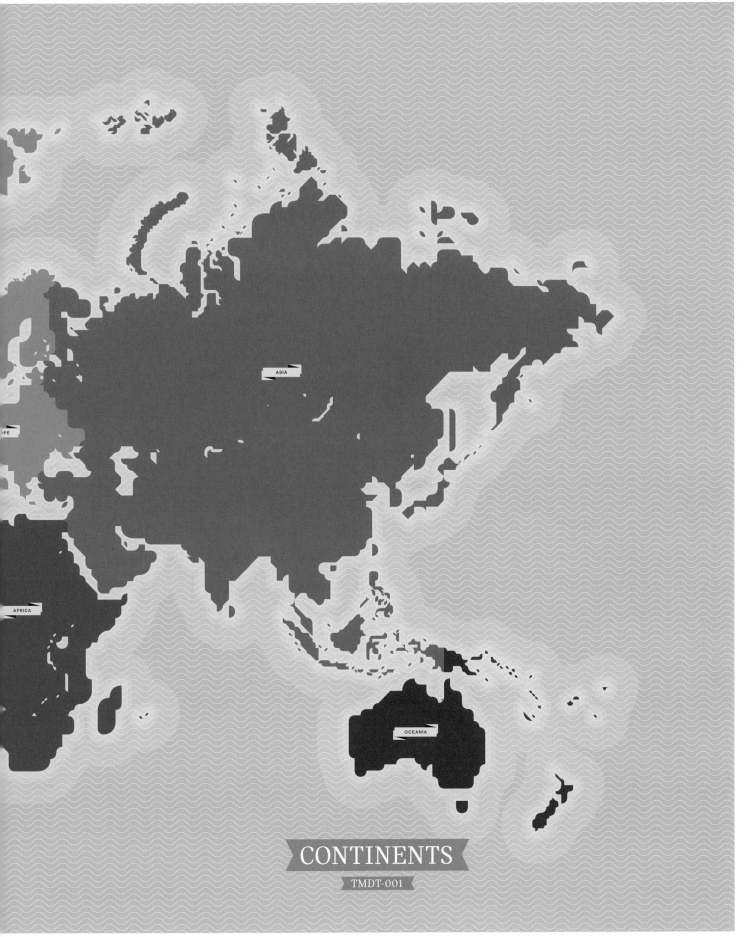

ASIA

PE

AFRICA

OCEANIA

CONTINENTS

TMDT-001

Greenland

Iceland

Canada

United Kingdom
Nethe
Ireland
Belgium
Lux
Switzerland
Liechtenstein
France
Bosn
Portugal   Spain

United States

Morocco

Algeria

Western Sahara

Mexico   Guatemala   Cuba   Dominican Republic   Mauritania
Belize   Guadeloupe   Mali
El Salvador   Haiti   Senegal   Burkina Faso
Honduras   Puerto Rico   Gambia   Benin
Nicaragua   Venezuela   Suriname   Guinea Bissau   Togo
Costa Rica   Panama   Guyana   Guinea   Ghana
Colombia   French Guiana   Sierra Leone   Liberia   Came
Galapagos Islands   Ecuador   Ivory Coast

Peru   Brazil

Bolivia

Chile   Paraguay

Uruguay

Argentina

Falkland Islands

COUNTRIES

TMDT-002

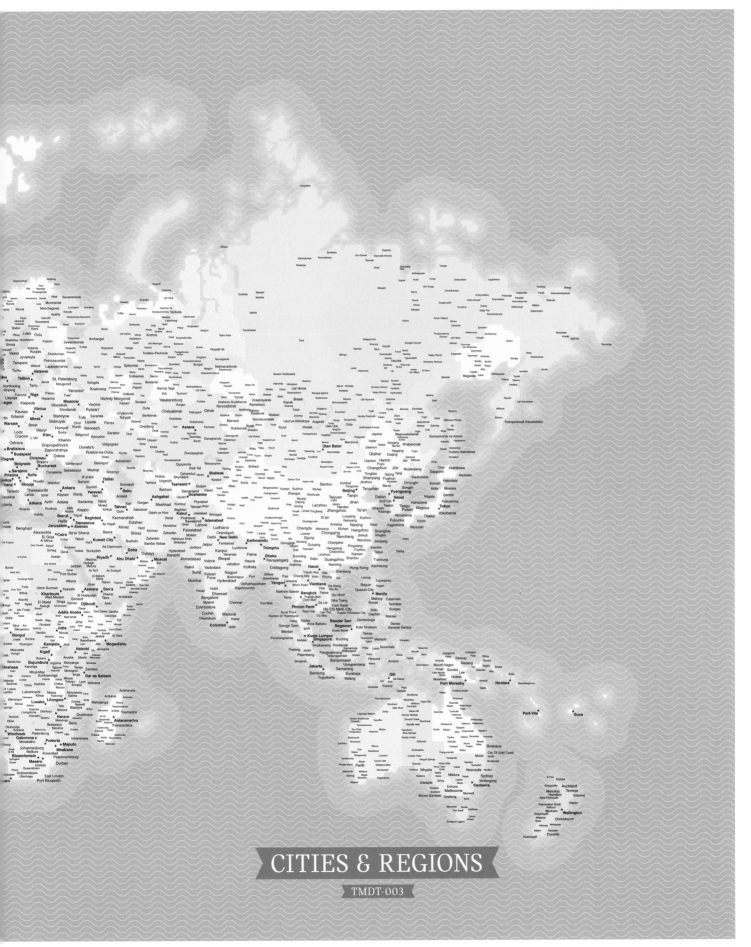

CITIES & REGIONS

TMDT-003

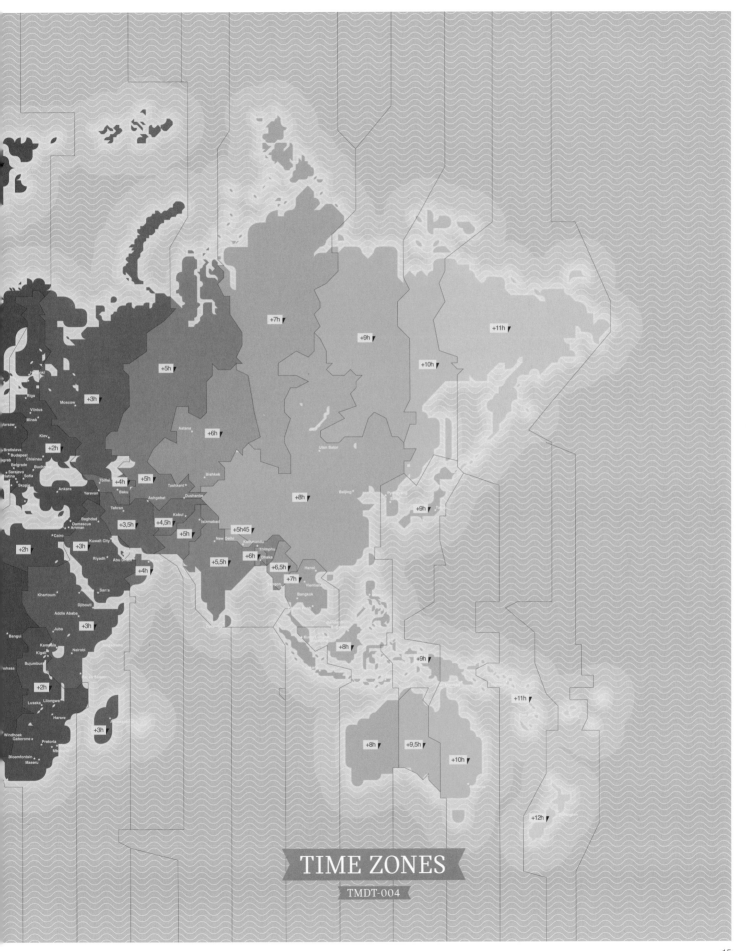

TIME ZONES

TMDT-004

15

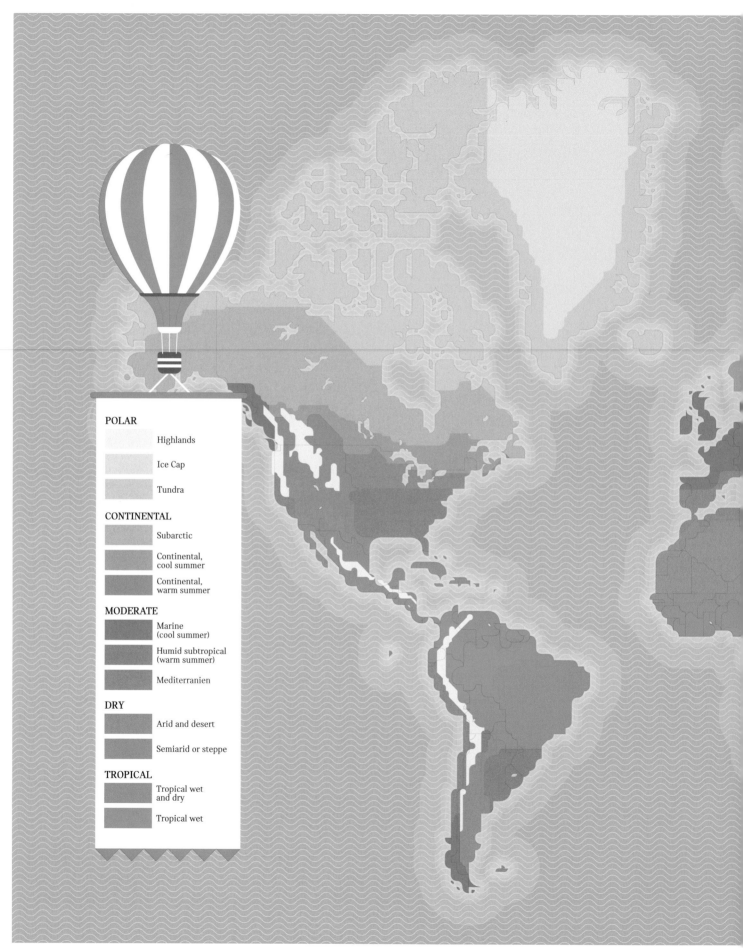

POLAR
- Highlands
- Ice Cap
- Tundra

CONTINENTAL
- Subarctic
- Continental, cool summer
- Continental, warm summer

MODERATE
- Marine (cool summer)
- Humid subtropical (warm summer)
- Mediterranien

DRY
- Arid and desert
- Semiarid or steppe

TROPICAL
- Tropical wet and dry
- Tropical wet

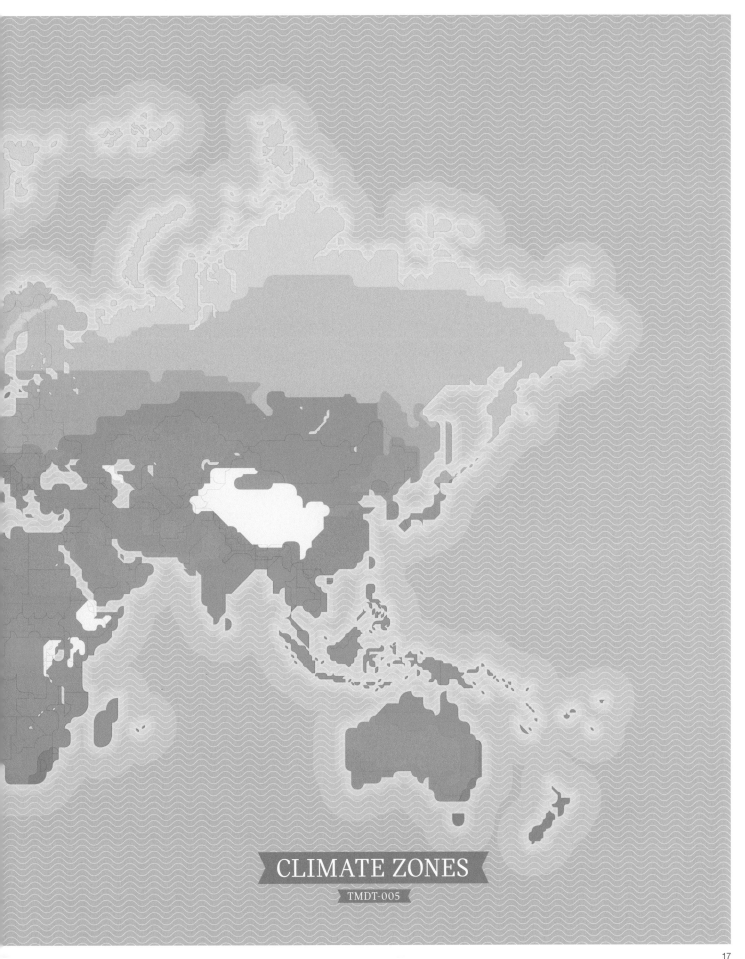

CLIMATE ZONES

TMDT-005

SPITSBERGE

EAST GREENLAND CURRENT

WEST GREENLAND CURRENT

NORWEGIAN CO

IRNINGER CURRENT

OYASHIO

ALASKA CURRENT

LABRADOR CURRENT

SUBARCTIC CURRENT

NORTH ATLANTIC CURRENT

DAVIDSON CURRENT

NORTH PACIFIC CURRENT

UROSHIO EXTENSION

GULFSTREAM

LORDA CURRENT

CALIFORNIA CURRENT

ANTILLES CURRENT

CANARY CURRENT

NORTH EQUATORIAL CURRENT

NORTH EQUATORIAL CURRENT

EQUATORIAL COUNTER CURRENT

EQUATORIAL COUNTER CURRENT

SOUTH EQUATORIAL CURRENT

SOUTH EQUATORIAL CURRENT

BRAZIL CURRENT

PERU CURRENT

BENGUE

FALKLAND CURRENT

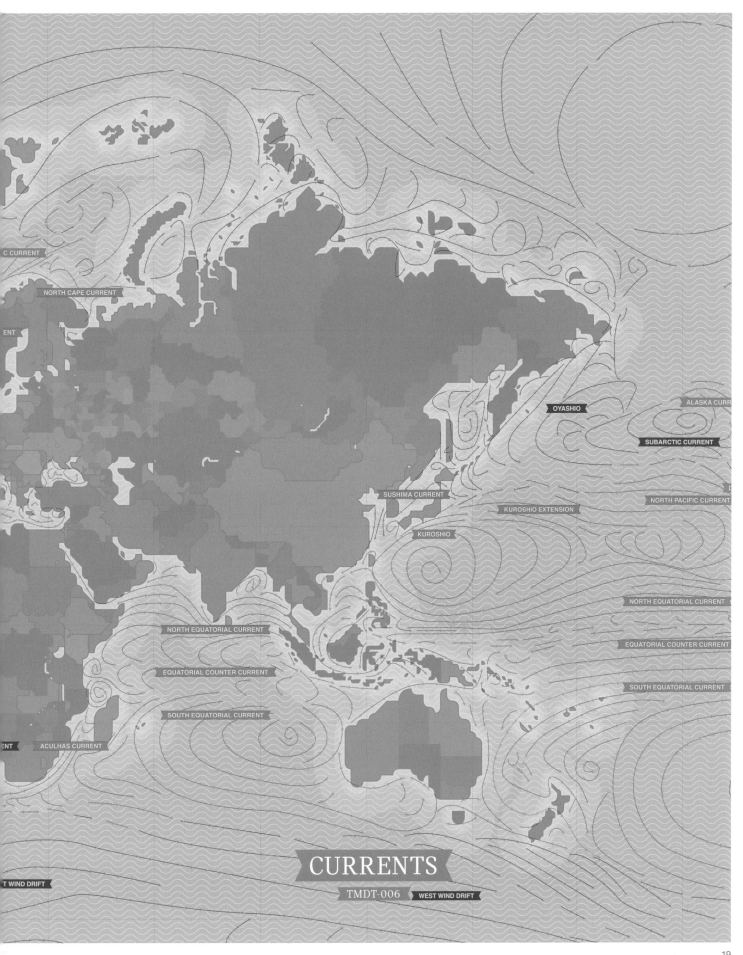

CURRENTS

TMDT-006 · WEST WIND DRIFT

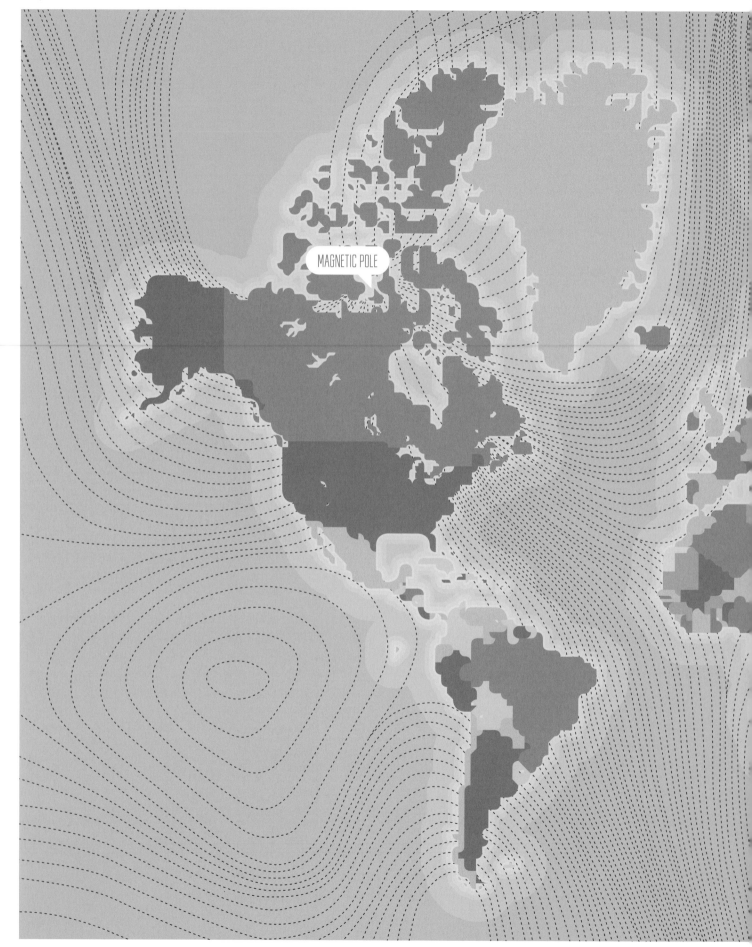

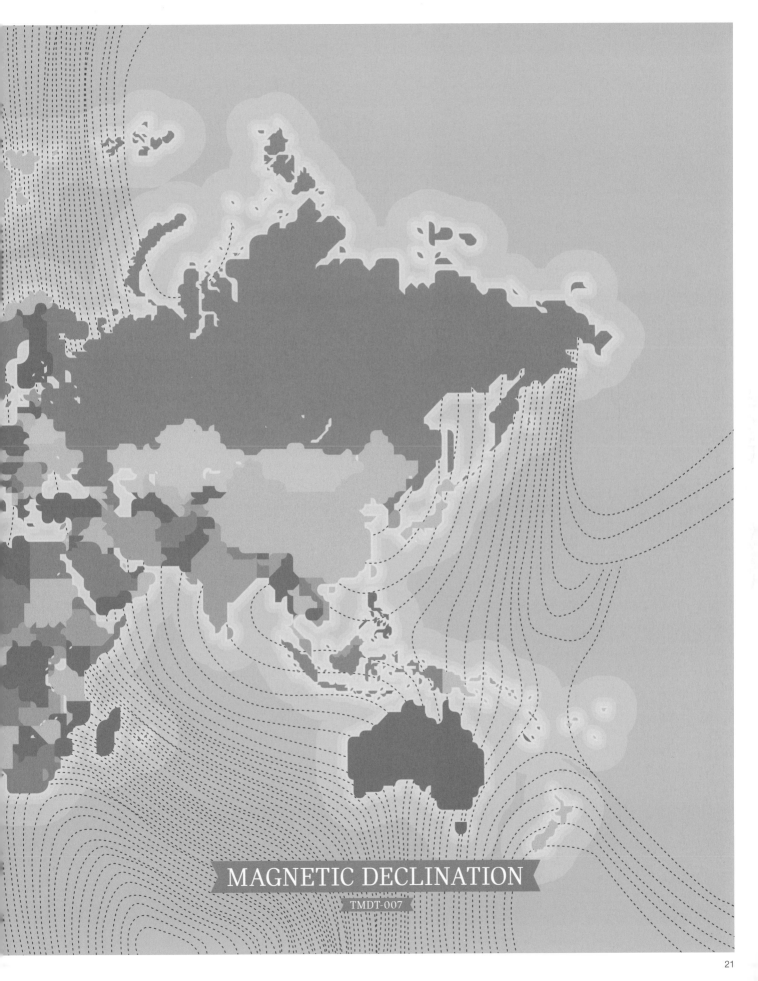

MAGNETIC DECLINATION

TMDT-007

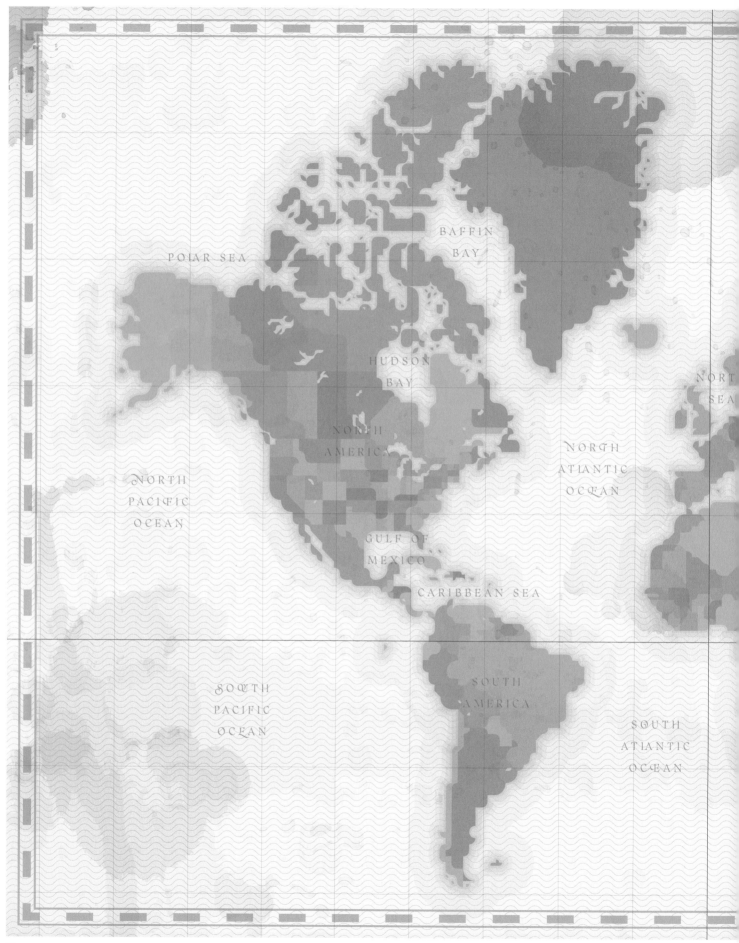

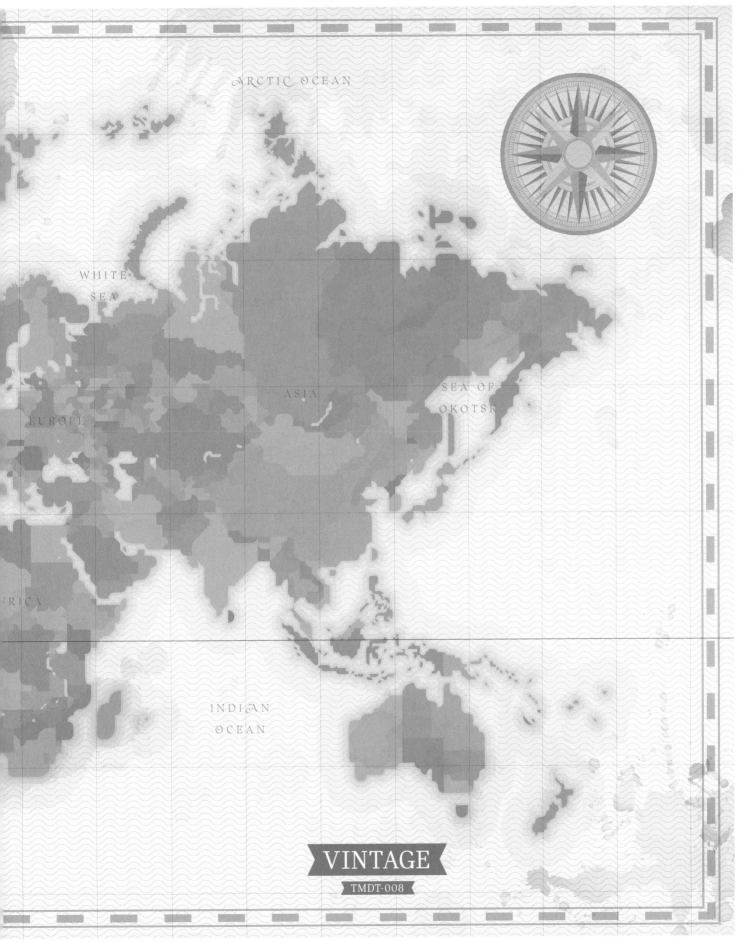

ARCTIC OCEAN

WHITE
SEA

ASIA

SEA OF
OKOTSK

EUROPE

FRICA

INDIAN
OCEAN

VINTAGE

TMDT-008

COUNTRÍES

BRAZIL

AIRPORT

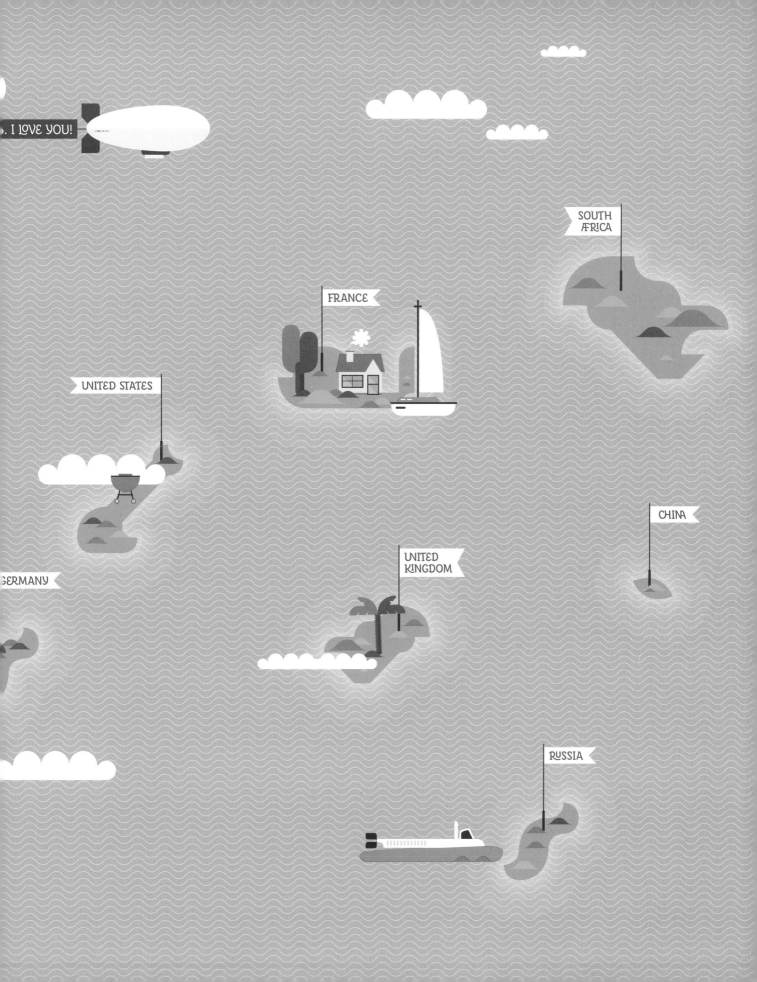

UNITED STATES of AMERICA

The United States is comprised of 50 states that vary in shape and size, ranging from 4 km² (Rhode Island) to 1,717,856 km² (Alaska). The U.S.A.'s climate and geography differ greatly from state to state, and it is the home of an extremely diverse population.

AREA	9,826,675 km²	TIME ZONE	(UTC-5 to -10)
POPULATION	318,047,000 (2013 estimate)		(UTC-4 to -10) Summer (DST)
CURRENCY	United States dollar ($)	CALLING CODE	+1

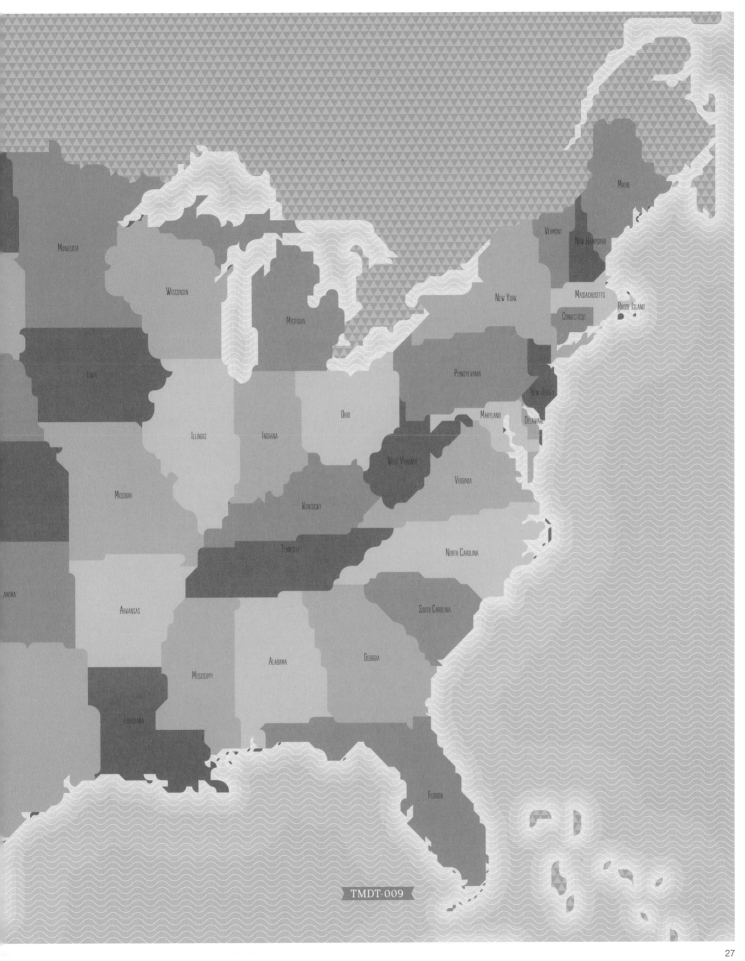

TMDT-009

27

TMDT-010

TMDT-011

TMDT-012

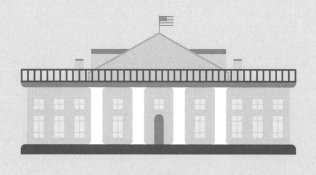

TMDT-013

TMDT-014

TMDT-015

TMDT-016

TMDT-017

TMDT-018

TMDT-019

TMDT-020

TMDT-021

TMDT-022

TMDT-023

HAPPY INDEPENDENCE DAY 4TH JULY

TMDT-035

TMDT-036

TMDT-037

NEW YORK

New York City is the most densely populated city in the United States. While it is not the political capital of the country, it is the cultural and financial center of the U.S.A., if not the world.

AREA				
	• Total	1.214 km²	• Metro	34.490 km²
	• Land	789 km²	POPULATION	8.405.837 (2013 estimate)
	• Water	425 km²	DENSITY	10.725.4 / km²

MANHATTAN

1 Battery Park City. Tribeca
2 Greenwich Village. Soho
3 Lower East Side. Chinatown
4 Chelsea. Clinton
5 Midtown Business District
6 Stuyvesant Town. Turtle Bay
7 West Side. Upper West Side
8 Upper East Side
9 Manhattanville. Hamilton Heights
10 Central Harlem
11 East Harlem
12 Washington Heights. Inwood

THE BRONX

1 Melrose. Mott Haven. Port Morris
2 Hunts Point. Longwood
3 Morrisania. Crotona Park East
4 Highbridge. Concourse Village
5 University Hts.. Fordham. Mt. Hope
6 East Tremont. Belmont
7 Bedford Park. Norwood. Fordham
8 Riverdale. Kingsbridge. Marble Hill
9 Soundview. Parkchester
10 Throgs Nk.. Co-op City. Pelham Bay
11 Pelham Pkwy. Morris Park. Laconia
12 Wakefield. Williamsbridge

QUEENS

1 Astoria. Long Island City
2 Sunnyside. Woodside
3 Jackson Heights. North Corona
4 Elmhurst. South Corona
5 Ridgewood. Glendale. Maspeth
6 Forest Hills. Rego Park
7 Flushing. Bay Terrace
8 Fresh Meadows. Briarwood
9 Woodhaven. Richmond Hill
10 Ozone Park. Howard Beach
11 Bayside. Douglaston. Little Neck
12 Jamaica. St. Albans. Hollis
13 Queens Village. Rosedale
14 The Rockaways. Broad Channel

STATEN ISLAND

1 Stapleton. Port Richmond
2 New Springville. South Beach
3 Tottenville. Woodrow. Great Kills

BROOKLYN

1 Williamsburg. Greenpoint
2 Brooklyn Heights. Fort Greene
3 Bedford Stuyvesant
4 Bushwick
5 East New York. Starrett City
6 Park Slope. Carroll Gardens
7 Sunset Park. Windsor Terrace
8 Crown Heights North
9 Crown Heights South. Wingate
10 Bay Ridge. Dyker Heights
11 Bensonhurst. Bath Beach
12 Borough Park. Ocean Parkway
13 Coney Island. Brighton Beach
14 Flatbush. Midwood
15 Sheepshead Bay. Gerritsen Beach
16 Brownsville. Ocean Hill
17 East Flatbush. Rugby. Farragut
18 Canarsie. Flatlands

AIRPORTS

A John F. Kennedy
B La Guardia

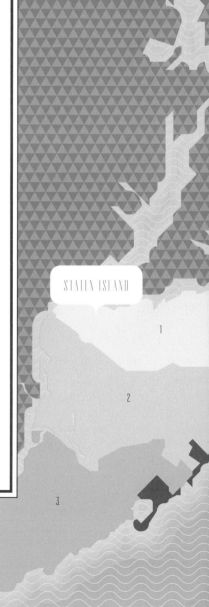

STATEN ISLAND

1

2

3

MANHATTAN

The island of Manhattan is the smallest borough of New York City. yet it has the biggest population of all five boroughs. Some of its most famous monuments include the Empire State Building. Rockefeller Center. and One World Trade Center (formerly known as the Freedom Tower) which is now the tallest building in the Western hemisphere.

AREA	87.5 km²
POPULATION	1.619.090 (2012 estimate)
DENSITY	27.227.1 / km²

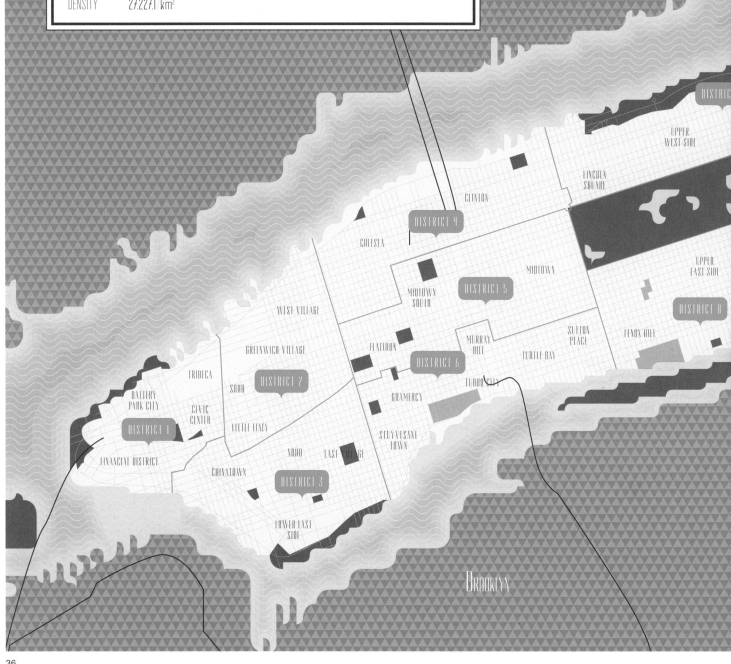

DISTRIC

UPPER
WEST SIDE

LINCOLN
SQUARE

CLINTON

DISTRICT 4

CHELSEA

MIDTOWN

UPPER
EAST SIDE

MIDTOWN
SOUTH

DISTRICT 5

WEST VILLAGE

DISTRICT 8

SUTTON
PLACE

LENOX HILL

MURRAY
HILL

GREENWICH VILLAGE

TURTLE BAY

FLATIRON

DISTRICT 6

TRIBECA

DISTRICT 2

TUDOR CITY

SOHO

BATTERY
PARK CITY

GRAMERCY

CIVIC
CENTER

DISTRICT 1

LITTLE ITALY

STUYVESANT
TOWN

NOHO

EAST VILLAGE

FINANCIAL DISTRICT

CHINATOWN

DISTRICT 3

LOWER EAST
SIDE

BROOKLYN

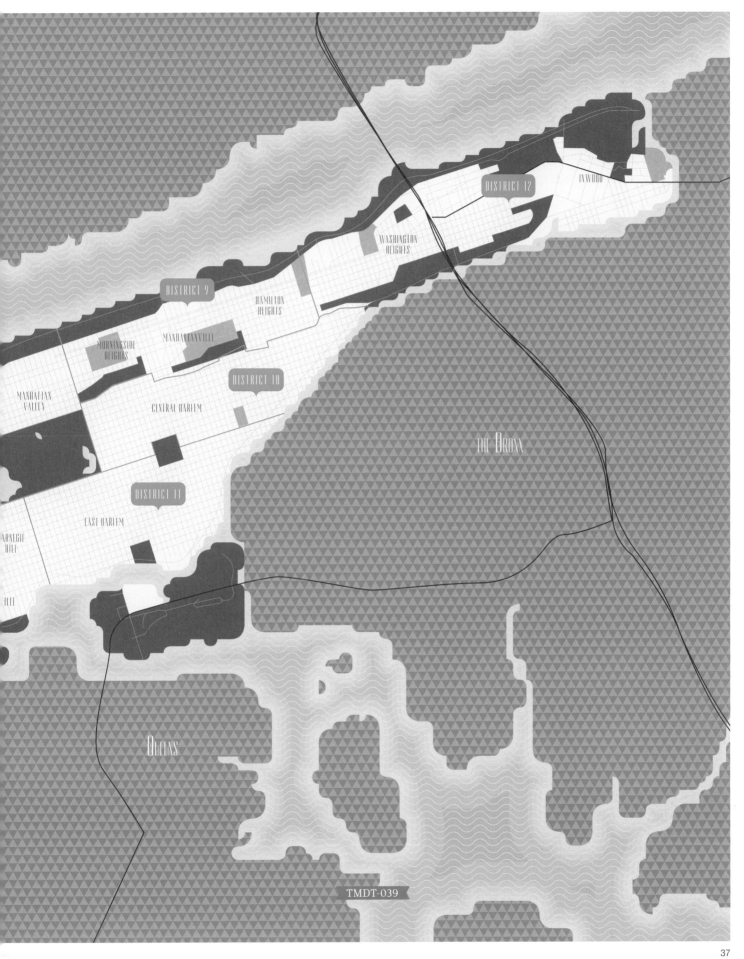

DISTRICT 12

INWOOD

WASHINGTON
HEIGHTS

DISTRICT 9

HAMILTON
HEIGHTS

MORNINGSIDE
HEIGHTS

MANHATTANVILLE

DISTRICT 10

MANHATTAN
VALLEY

CENTRAL HARLEM

THE BRONX

DISTRICT 11

EAST HARLEM

CARNEGIE
HILL

FLEE

QUEENS

TMDT-039

TMDT-040

TMDT-041

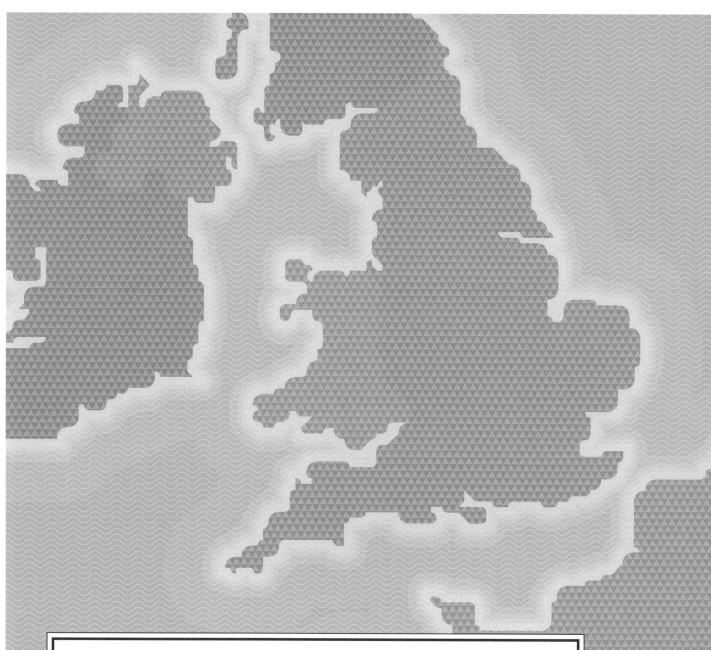

GERMANY

Beyond being known as the country of beer and sausages, Germany has also been an intellectual hub for many centuries, producing giants in the fields of philosophy, music, and letters. Germany is also Europe's largest economy and most populous country.

AREA	357,168 km²	TIME ZONE	CET (UTC 1)
POPULATION	80,219,695 (2011 census)		CEST (UTC 2) Summer (DST)
CURRENCY	Euro (€)	INTL. CODE	49

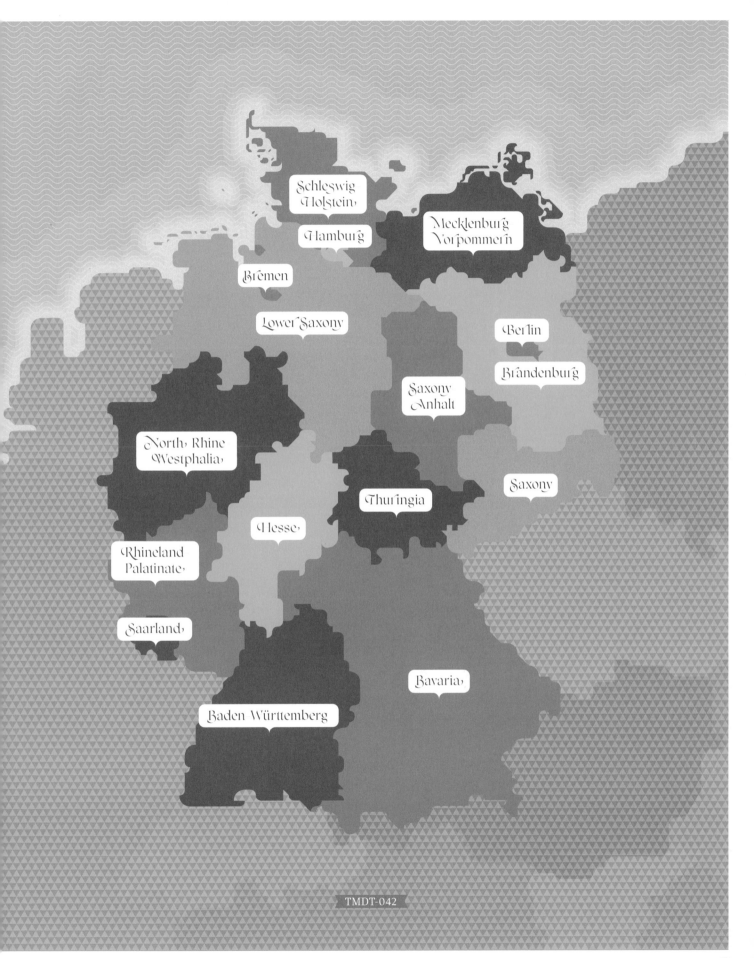

TMDT-043   TMDT-044

TMDT-045

TMDT-046

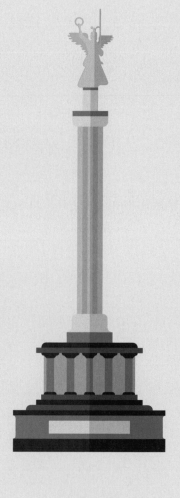

TMDT-047

TMDT-048

TMDT-049

TMDT-050

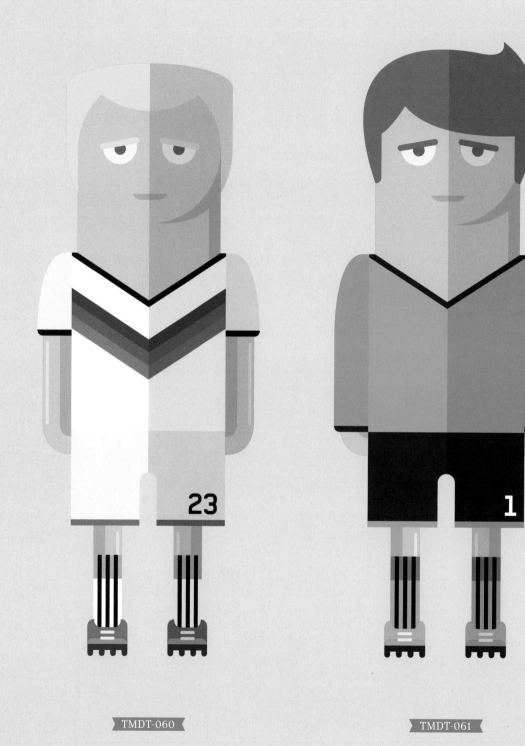

TMDT-060

TMDT-061

54

TMDT-062

74

TMDT-063

90

TMDT-064

14

TMDT-065

BERLIN

Berlin, Germany's capital, is the greenest city in Europe with sprawling parks, lakes, and forests that span over one third of its area. Berlin's historical legacy can be felt in the diverse architecture of the city, mixing old and new with ease.

AREA	891.85 km²
POPULATION	3,415,091 (2013 census)
DENSITY	3,800 km²

LOCALITIES (ORTSTEILE)

101 Mitte	505 Gatow	910 Köpenick
102 Moabit	506 Kladow	911 Friedrichshagen
103 Hansaviertel	507 Hakenfelde	912 Rahnsdorf
104 Tiergarten	508 Falkenhagener Feld	913 Grünau
105 Wedding	509 Wilhelmstadt	914 Müggelheim
106 Gesundbrunnen	601 Steglitz	915 Schmöckwitz
201 Friedrichshain	602 Lichterfelde	1001 Marzahn
202 Kreuzberg	603 Lankwitz	1002 Biesdorf
301 Prenzlauer Berg	604 Zehlendorf	1003 Kaulsdorf
302 Weißensee	605 Dahlem	1004 Mahlsdorf
303 Blankenburg	606 Nikolassee	1005 Hellersdorf
304 Heinersdorf	607 Wannsee	1101 Friedrichsfelde
305 Karow	701 Schöneberg	1102 Karlshorst
306 Stadtrandsiedlung	702 Friedenau	1103 Lichtenberg
307 Pankow	703 Tempelhof	1104 Falkenberg
308 Blankenfelde	704 Mariendorf	1106 Malchow
309 Buch	705 Marienfelde	1107 Wartenberg
310 Französisch Buchholz	706 Lichtenrade	1108 Neu Hohenschönhausen
311 Niederschönhausen	801 Neukölln	1110 Alt Hohenschönhausen
312 Rosenthal	802 Britz	1111 Fennpfuhl
313 Wilhelmsruh	803 Buckow	1112 Rummelsburg
401 Charlottenburg	804 Rudow	1201 Reinickendorf
402 Wilmersdorf	805 Gropiusstadt	1202 Tegel
403 Schmargendorf	901 Alt Treptow	1203 Konradshöhe
404 Grunewald	902 Plänterwald	1204 Heiligensee
405 Westend	903 Baumschulenweg	1205 Frohnau
406 Charlottenburg Nord	904 Johannisthal	1206 Hermsdorf
407 Halensee	905 Niederschöneweide	1207 Waidmannslust
501 Spandau	906 Altglienicke	1208 Lübars
502 Haselhorst	907 Adlershof	1209 Wittenau
503 Siemensstadt	908 Bohnsdorf	1210 Märkisches Viertel
504 Staaken	909 Oberschöneweide	1211 Borsigwalde

NICKEN
DORF

PANKOW

1205

309

1206

1208

308

310

1207

1210

305

1209

312

LICHTEN-
BERG

1211

313

303

1107

1201

311

306

1106

1104

307

304

1108

MARZAHN
HELLERSDORF

302

105

106

110

1001

MITTE

301

1005

102

FRIEDRICHSHAIN–
KREUZBERG

103

104

201

1103

302

202

112

1101

1002

1004

202

101

1003

701

1102

TREPTOW
KÖPENIHCK

702

703

801

902

903

601

704

802

803

905

907

901

TEGLITZ
ILENDORF

602

603

804

906

912

705

904

914

706

NEUKÖLLN

908

913

TEMPELHOF
SCHÖNEBERG

TMDT-066

49

SCOTLAND

N. IRELAND

NORTH EAST
ENGLAND

NORTH WEST
ENGLAND

YORKSHIRE
AND THE
HUMBER

EAST MIDLANDS

WEST
MIDLANDS

WALES

EAST OF ENGLAND

GREATER
LONDON

SOUTH WEST ENGLAND

SOUTH EAST ENGLAND

ENGLAND

TMDT-067

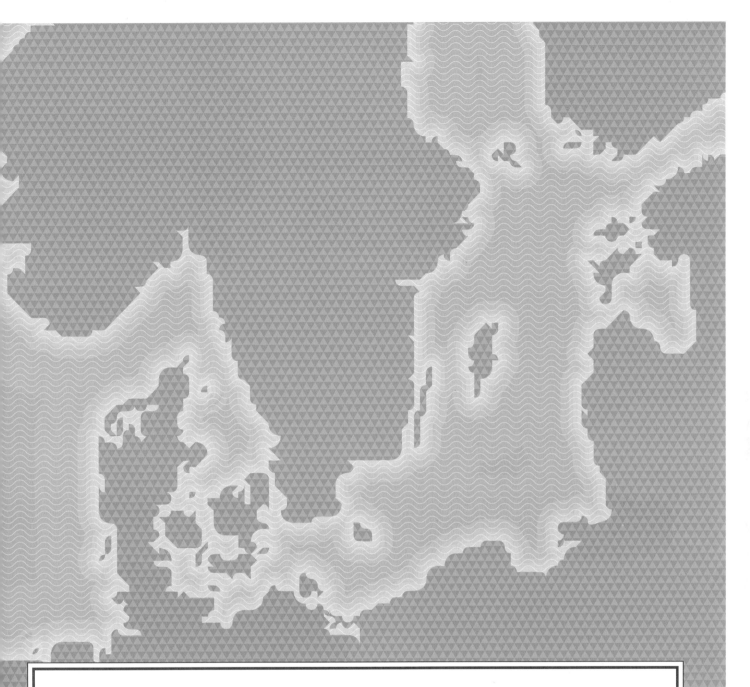

UNITED KINGDOM

The United Kingdom refers to four countries: England, Scotland, Wales, and Northern Ireland. It is governed by a constitutional monarchy with a parliamentary system, and Queen Elizabeth II has been at its head since 1952.

AREA	243,610 km²	TIME ZONE	GMT (UTC)
POPULATION	63,181,775 (2011 census)		BST (UTC+1)
CURRENCY	Pound sterling (£)	INTL. CODE	+44

TMDT-068

TMDT-069

TMDT-070

TMDT-071

TMDT-072

TMDT-073

TMDT-074

TMDT-075

TMDT-076

TMDT-077

TMDT-078

TMDT-079

TMDT-080

TMDT-081

53

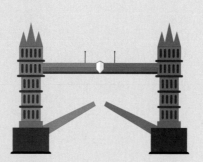

TMDT-083

TMDT-084

TMDT-082

TMDT-085

TMDT-086

TMDT-087

TMDT-088

TMDT-089

TMDT-090

TMDT-091

TMDT-092

TMDT-093

TMDT-094

TMDT-095

UNDERGROUND

TMDT-096

TMDT-097

OUTER LONDON
BOROUGHS

Barnet

Harrow

Brent

Hillingdon

Ealing

H&F

Hounslow

Wands

Richmond
upon
Thames

Mer

Kingston
upon
Thames

LONDON

London is both the capital of England as well as the
United Kingdom. It is a leading global city and one of the
financial centers of the world. With over eight million
people, London is the most populated city within the
European Union.

AREA	1,572.00 km²
POPULATION	8,308,369
DENSITY	5,285/km²

Enfield

Haringey

Waltham Forest

Redbridge

Havering

n

Islington

Hackney

Barking & Dagenham

Newham

Tower Hamlets

est- City nster

Greenwich

South- wark

Bexley

Lambeth

Lewisham

INNER LONDON BOROUGHS

Bromley

Croydon

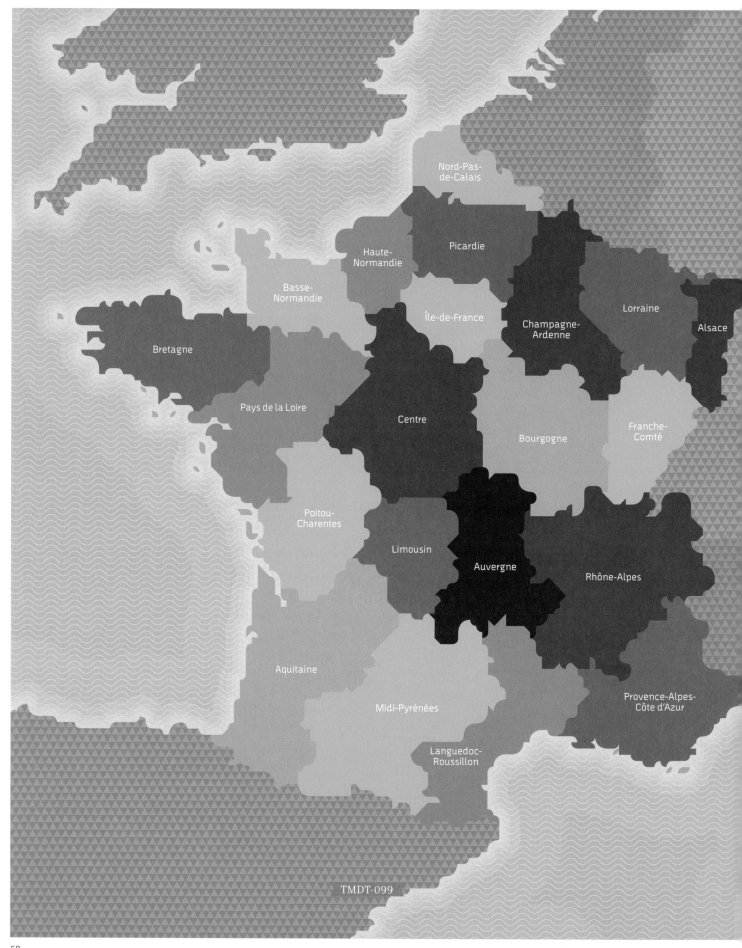

Nord-Pas-de-Calais

Picardie

Haute-Normandie

Basse-Normandie

Bretagne

Pays de la Loire

Île-de-France

Champagne-Ardenne

Lorraine

Alsace

Centre

Bourgogne

Franche-Comté

Poitou-Charentes

Limousin

Auvergne

Rhône-Alpes

Aquitaine

Midi-Pyrénées

Provence-Alpes-Côte d'Azur

Languedoc-Roussillon

TMDT-099

Corse

FRANCE

France, often referred to as the Hexagon due to its shape, is the largest country in the European Union by area. It is one of the world's leading centers for culture, which ties into its high quality of life with great emphasis on art, music, and food. France is also one of the five permanent members of the UN Security Council within the United Nations, which it helped to found in 1945.

AREA	640,679 km²	TIME ZONE	CET (UTC+1)
POPULATION	66,616,416		CEST (UTC+2) Summer (DST)
CURRENCY	Euro (€)	INTL. CODE	+33

TMDT-100

TMDT-101

TMDT-102

TMDT-103

TMDT-104

TMDT-105

TMDT-106

TMDT-107

TMDT-108

TMDT-109

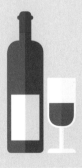

TMDT-110

TMDT-111

TMDT-112

TMDT-113

64

PARIS

Paris, the capital of France, is built in the shape of a coil around the Seine River. It lies in the heart of the Île-de France, also referred to as the Paris Region, and is comprised of twenty neighborhoods called arrondissements.

AREA	• Urban	2,844.8 km²		POPULATION	2,249,975
	• Metro	17,174.4 km²		DENSITY	21.347/km²

QUARTIERS

1st	Saint-Germain-l'Auxerrois	28th	Gros-Caillou	54th	Parc Montsouris
2nd	Les Halles			55th	Petit-Montrouge
3rd	Palais-Royal	29th	Champs-Élysées	56th	Plaisance
4th	Place-Vendôme	30th	Faubourg-du-Roule		
		31st	La Madeleine	57th	Saint-Lambert
5th	Gaillon	32nd	Europe	58th	Necker
6th	Vivienne			59th	Grenelle
7th	Mail	33rd	Saint-Georges	60th	Javel
8th	Bonne-Nouvelle	34th	Chaussée-d'Antin		
		35th	Faubourg-Montmartre	61st	Auteuil
9th	Arts-et-Métiers	36th	Rochechouart	62nd	La Muette
10th	Enfants-Rouges			63rd	Porte-Dauphine
11th	Archives	37th	Saint-Vincent-de-Paul	64th	Chaillot
12th	Sainte-Avoye	38th	Porte-Saint-Denis		
		39th	Porte-Saint-Martin	65th	Les Ternes
13th	Saint-Merri	40th	Hôpital-Saint-Louis	66th	Plaine Monceau
14th	Saint-Gervais			67th	Batignolles
15th	Arsenal	41st	Folie-Méricourt	68th	Épinettes
16th	Notre-Dame	42nd	Saint-Ambroise		
		43rd	La Roquette	69th	Grandes-Carrières
17th	Quartier Saint-Victor	44th	Sainte-Marguerite	70th	Clignancourt
18th	Jardin-des-Plantes			71st	Goutte-d'Or
19th	Val-de-Grâce	45th	Bel-Air	72nd	La Chapelle
20th	Sorbonne	46th	Picpus		
		47th	Bercy	73rd	La Villette
21st	Monnaie	48th	Quinze-Vingts	74th	Pont-de-Flandres
22nd	Odéon			75th	Amérique
23rd	Notre-Dame-des-Champs	49th	Salpêtrière	76th	Combat
24th	Saint-Germain-des-Prés	50th	La Gare		
		51st	Maison-Blanche	77th	Belleville
25th	Saint-Thomas-d'Aquin	52nd	Croulebarbe	78th	Saint-Fargeau
26th	Les Invalides			79th	Père-Lachaise
27th	École-Militaire	53rd	Montparnasse	80th	Charonne

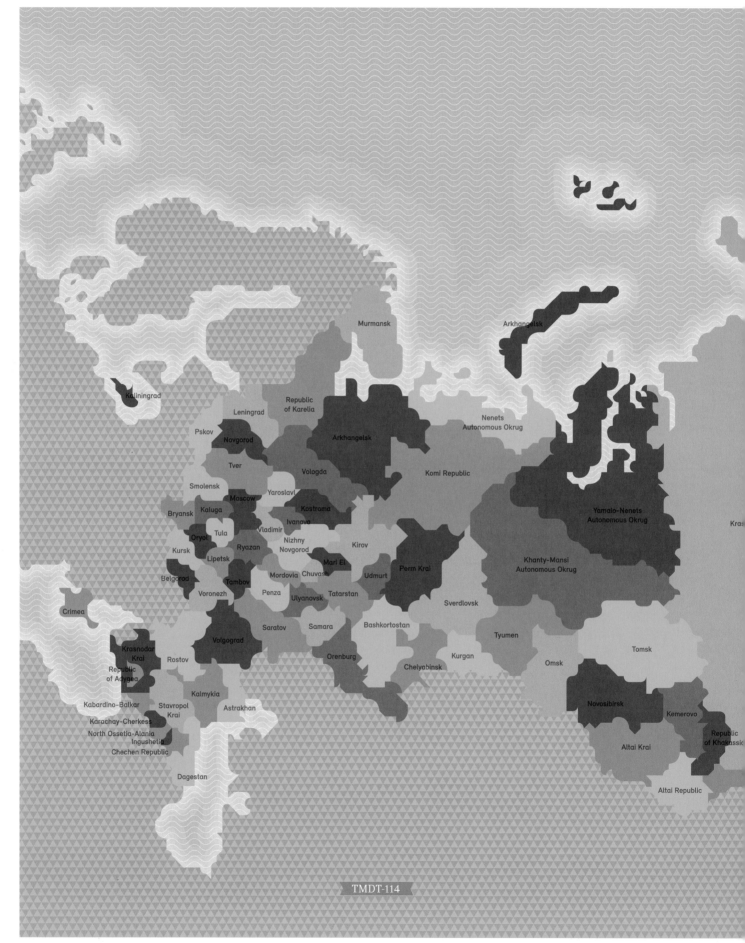

Kaliningrad

Murmansk

Arkhangelsk

Leningrad

Republic
of Karelia

Nenets
Autonomous Okrug

Pskov

Novgorod

Arkhangelsk

Tver

Vologda

Komi Republic

Smolensk

Yaroslavl

Moscow

Kostroma

Bryansk

Kaluga

Ivanovo

Yamalo-Nenets
Autonomous Okrug

Kras

Vladimir

Oryol

Tula

Nizhny
Novgorod

Kirov

Khanty-Mansi
Autonomous Okrug

Kursk

Ryazan

Perm Krai

Lipetsk

Mari El

Belgorod

Tambov

Mordovia

Chuvash

Udmurt

Voronezh

Penza

Ulyanovsk

Tatarstan

Sverdlovsk

Crimea

Saratov

Samara

Bashkortostan

Tyumen

Tomsk

Volgograd

Orenburg

Kurgan

Krasnodar
Krai

Rostov

Chelyabinsk

Omsk

Republic
of Adygea

Kalmykia

Novosibirsk

Kabardino-Balkar

Stavropol
Krai

Astrakhan

Kemerovo

Karachay-Cherkess

Republic
of Khakassia

North Ossetia-Alania
Ingushetia

Altai Krai

Chechen Republic

Dagestan

Altai Republic

TMDT-114

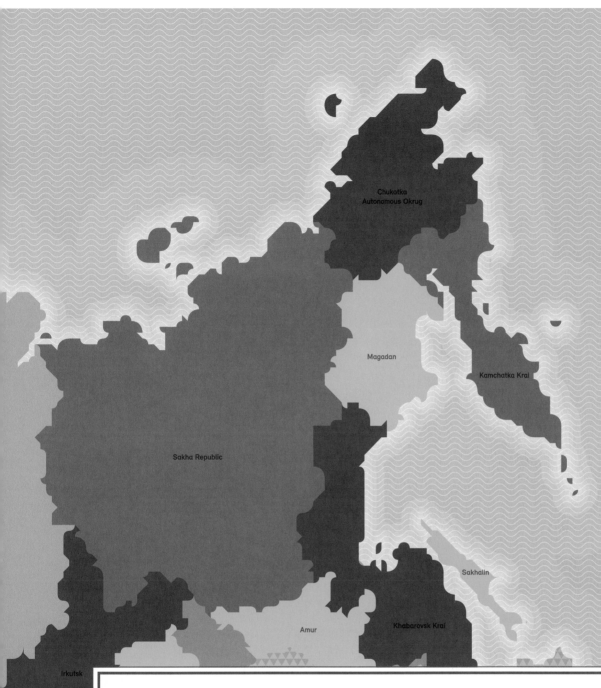

Chukotka
Autonomous Okrug

Magadan

Kamchatka Krai

Sakha Republic

Sakhalin

Amur

Khabarovsk Krai

Irkutsk

RUSSIA

Russia's area covers over one-eighth of the Earth's inhabited land, making it the
largest country in the world. Its diverse landscapes span across nine time zones.

AREA	17,098,242 km² (Crimea not included)	CURRENCY	Russian ruble (₽)
	17,125,242 km² (Crimea included)	TIME ZONE	(UTC+3 to +12)
POPULATION	143,700,000 (2014 estimate)	INTL. CODE	+7

TMDT-115   TMDT-116

TMDT-117

TMDT-118

TMDT-119

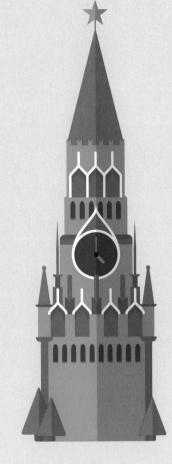

TMDT-122

TMDT-120

TMDT-121

TMDT-123

TMDT-124

TMDT-125

TMDT-126

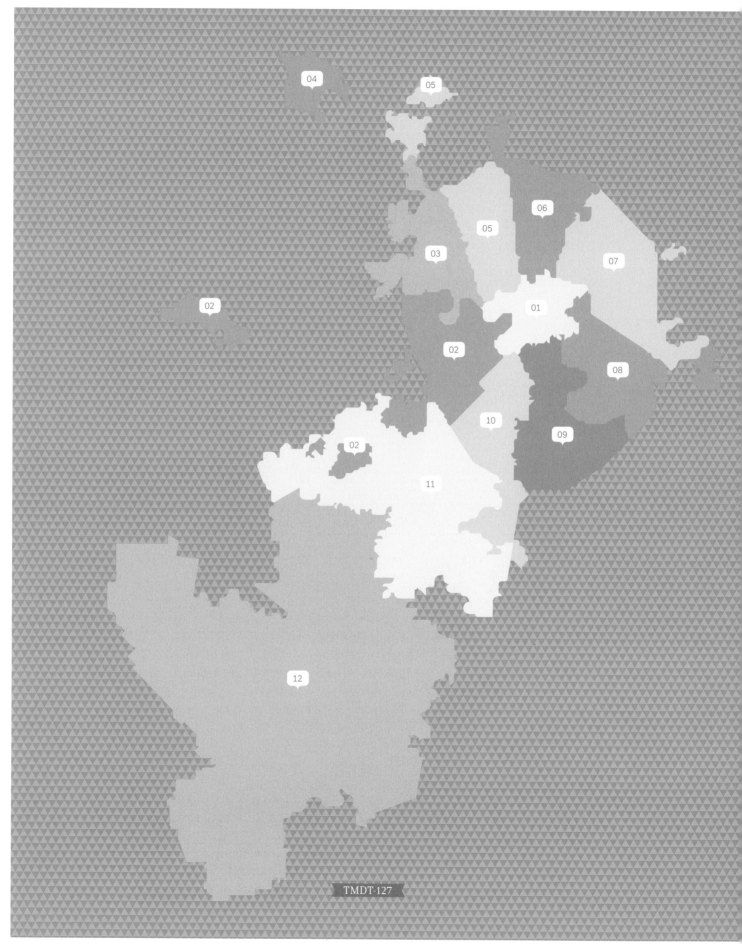

TMDT-127

MOSCOW

Moscow is the capital of Russia, as well as its most populated city. It is one of the world's most expensive cities and is home to the largest number of billionaires. Moscow is also one of the greenest capitals with vegetation (including the biggest forest in an urban area) covering 40% of its territory.

AREA	2,511 km^2
POPULATION	12,108,257 (2014 estimate)
DENSITY	4,581.24 /km^2

01. Central Administrative Okrug
02. Western Administrative Okrug
03. North-Western Administrative Okrug
04. Zelenograd
05. Northern Administrative Okrug
06. North-Eastern Administrative Okrug
07. Eastern Administrative Okrug
08. South-Eastern Administrative Okrug
09. Southern Administrative Okrug
10. South-Western Administrative Okrug
11. Novomoskovsky Administrative Okrug
12. Troitsky Administrative Okrug

Brazil

Brazil is the largest country in Latin America and the only one in both North and South America with Portuguese as its national language. It is one of the world's fastest growing economies and has been the world's prime producer of coffee for the past 150 years.

Area	8,515,767 km²	Currency	Real (R$)
Population	201,032,714 (2013 estimate)	Time zone	BRT (UTC-2 to -5)
Density	23.7/km2	Intl. code	+55

TMDT-128

75

TMDT-129

TMDT-130

TMDT-131

TMDT-132

TMDT-133

TMDT-134

TMDT-135

TMDT-136

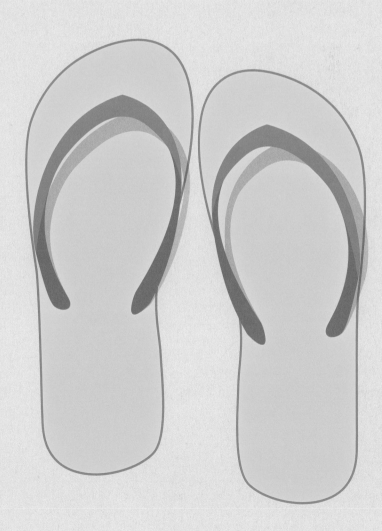

TMDT-137

TMDT-138

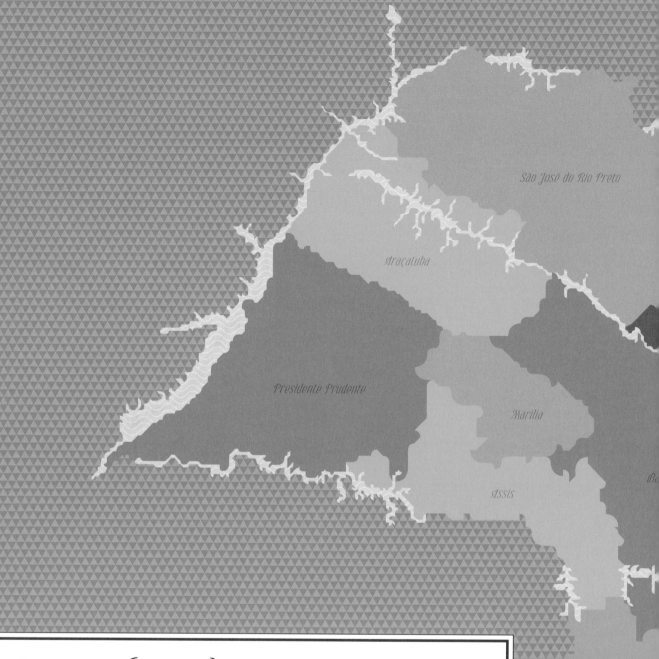

São José do Rio Preto

Araçatuba

Presidente Prudente

Marília

Assis

São Paulo

São Paulo is the largest city in the Southern hemisphere. Its weather is famously unreliable, and it is the host of the world's biggest gay pride parade. While it is not the capital of Brazil, São Paulo holds significant economic, cultural, and political power on a national scale.

Area	7,943,818 km²
Population	11,821,876 (2013 estimate)
Density	7,762.3/km²

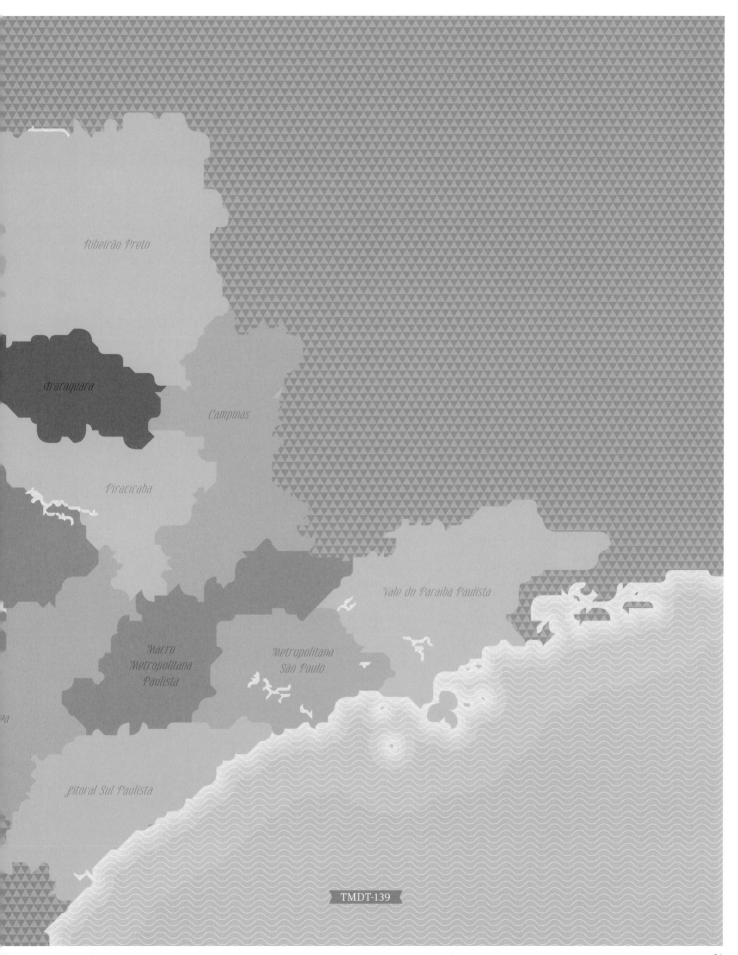

Ribeirão Preto

draraquara

Campinas

Piracicaba

Vale do Paraíba Paulista

Macro
Metropolitana
Paulista

Metropolitana
São Paulo

Litoral Sul Paulista

TMDT-139

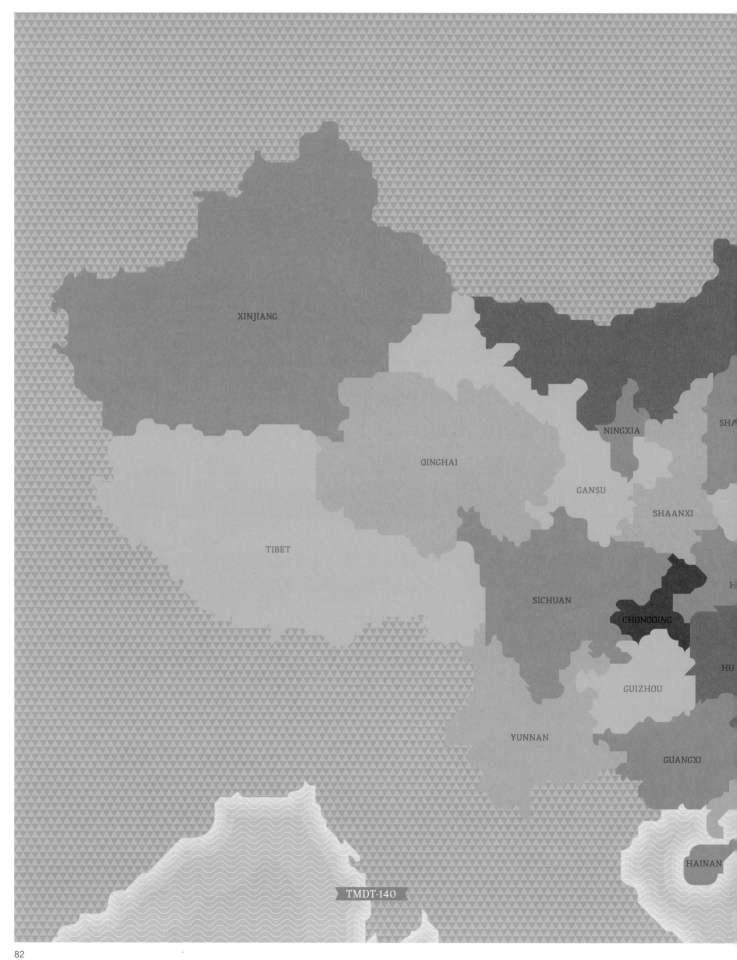

TMDT-140

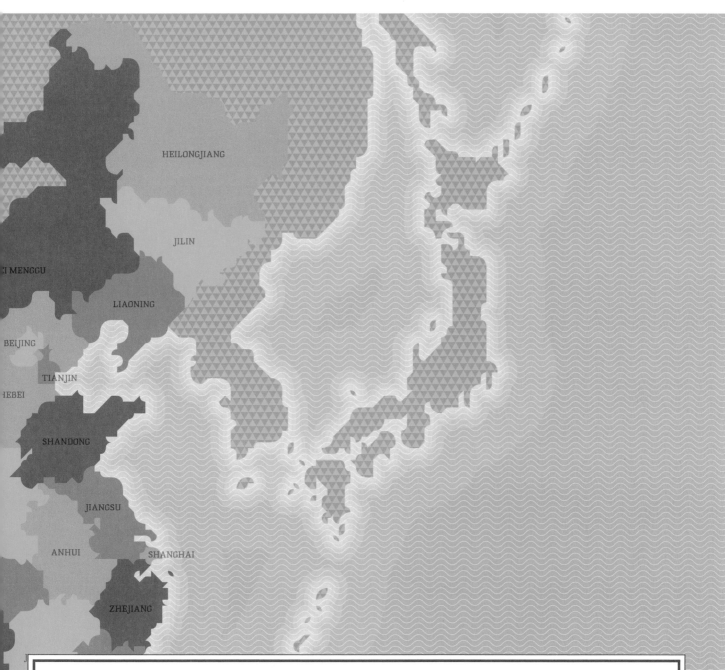

HEILONGJIANG

JILIN

CI MENGGU

LIAONING

BEIJING

TIANJIN

HEBEI

SHANDONG

JIANGSU

ANHUI

SHANGHAI

ZHEJIANG

UANG

CHINA

China is the Earth's most populated country, and the second biggest in area after Russia. Its imports and exports surpass any other country's, and its economy is the second largest in the world since 2013.

AREA	9,596,961 km²	CURRENCY	Renminbi (yuan)(¥)
POPULATION	1,339,724,852 (2010 census)	TIME ZONE	China Standard Time (UTC+8)
DENSITY	144/km²	INTL. CODE	+86

TMDT-141

TMDT-142

TMDT-143

TMDT-144

TMDT-145

TMDT-146

TMDT-147

TMDT-148

TMDT-149

TMDT-150

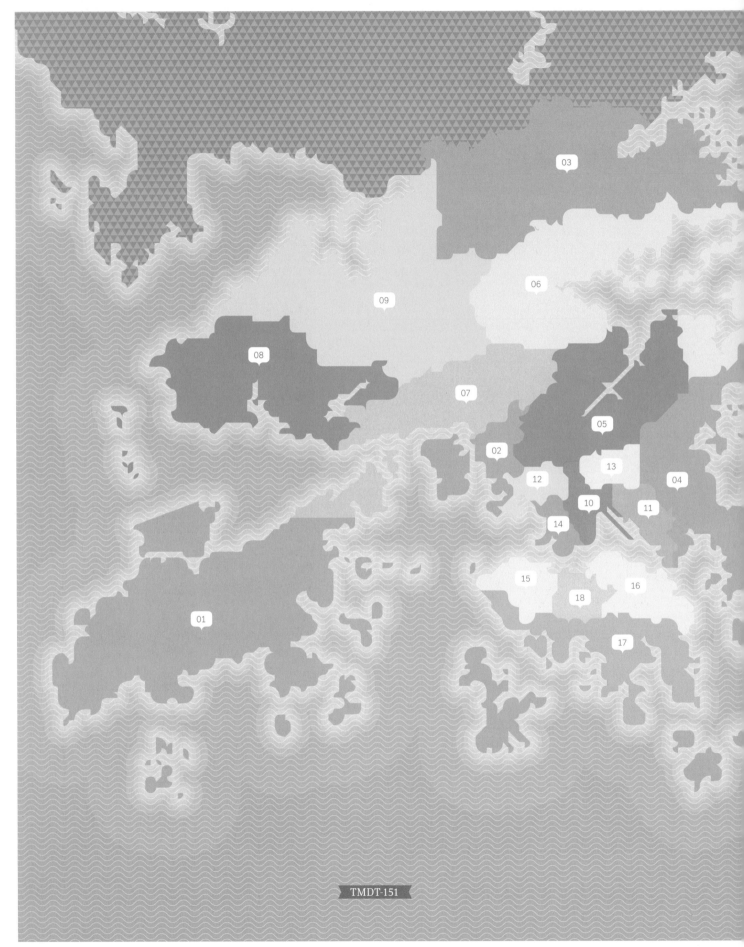

TMDT-151

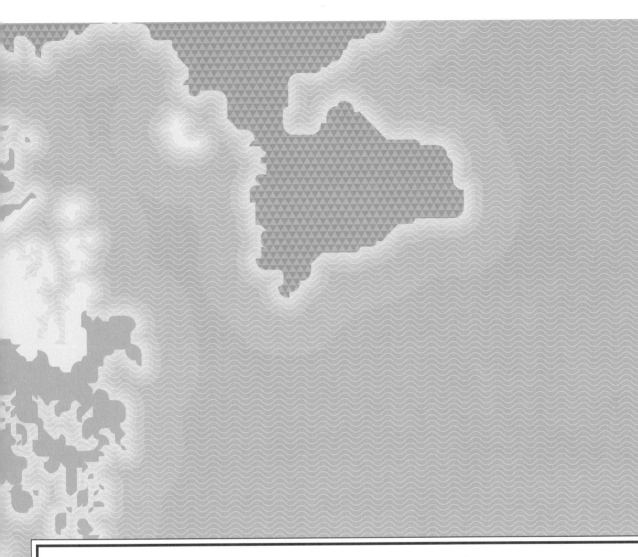

HONG KONG

A British colony in the past, Hong Kong is a Special Administrative Region of the People's Republic of China since 1997. Its political system is different from that of mainland China, and it is the world's third most important financial center after London and New York City.

AREA	1,104 km^2		DENSITY	6,544/km^2
POPULATION	7,184,000 (2013 estimate)		CURRENCY	Hong Kong dollar (HK$)

NEW TERRITORIES

01. Islands
02. Kwai Sing
03. North
04. Sai Kung
05. Sha Tin
06. Tai Po
07. Tsuen Wan
08. Tuen Mun
09. Yuen Long

KOWLOON
10. Shum Shui Po
11. Kowloon city
12. Kwun Tong
13. Wong Tai Sin
14. Yau Tsim Mong

HONG KONG ISLAND
15. Central and Western
16. Eastern
17. Southern
18. Wan Chai

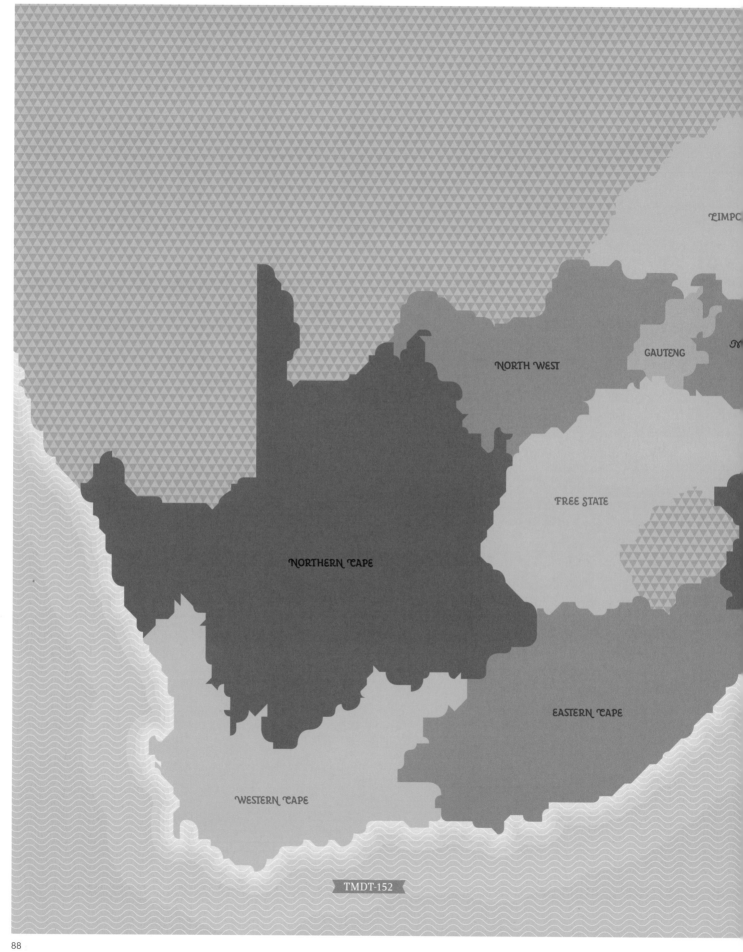

LIMPO

NORTH WEST

GAUTENG

N

FREE STATE

NORTHERN CAPE

EASTERN CAPE

WESTERN CAPE

TMDT-152

NGA

WAZULU-NATAL

SOUTH AFRICA

The Republic of South Africa is located on the southern-most tip of the African continent, and is composed of a variety of cultures and religions. It is one of the world's most multilingual countries as it has 11 official languages, with Afrikaans as the most widely spoken one.

AREA	1,221,037 km²	CURRENCY	South African rand (ZAR)
POPULATION	52,981,991 (2013 estimate)	TIME ZONE	SAST (UTC+2)
DENSITY	42.4/km²	INTL. CODE	+27

TMDT-153

TMDT-154

TMDT-155

TMDT-156

TMDT-157

TMDT-158

TMDT-159

TMDT-160

TMDT-161

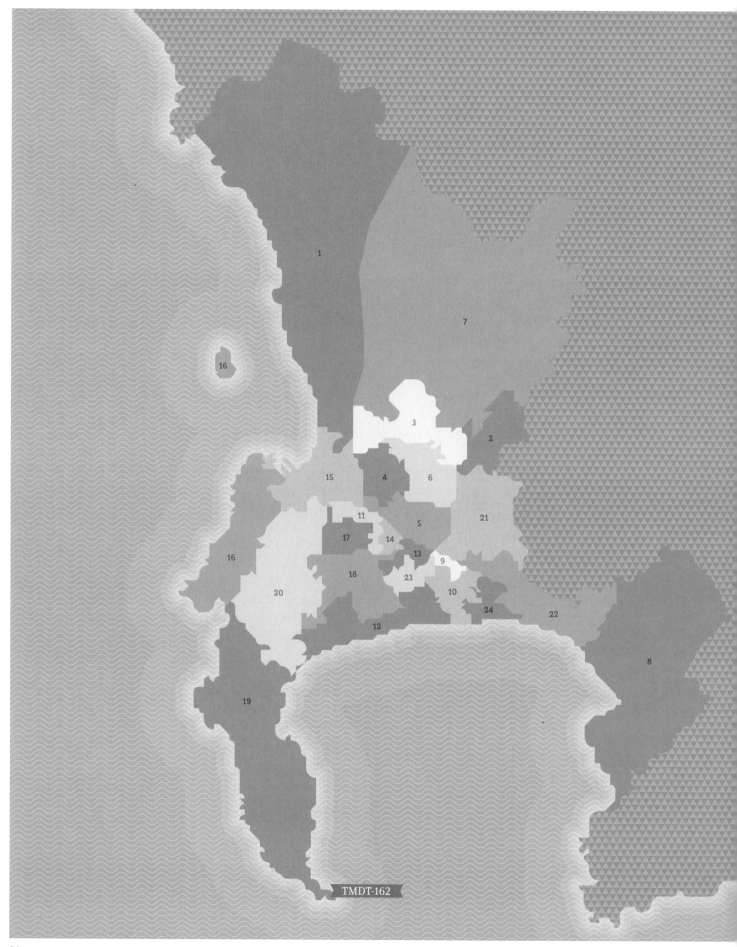

TMDT-162

CAPETOWN

Cape Town is the capital of the Republic of South Africa, and is one of the most multicultural cities in the world. In 2014, the International Council of Societies of Industrial Design named it the World Design Capital, and it was also deemed the best destination to visit by *The New York Times*.

AREA	2,445 km²
POPULATION	3,740,026 (2011 estimate)
DENSITY	1,500/km²

SUBCOUNCILS

1	Ward 4, 23, 29, 32, 104, 107	13	Ward 33, 34, 35, 36
2	Ward 6, 7, 8, 111	14	Ward 37, 38, 39, 40, 41
3	Ward 1, 3, 5, 70	15	Ward 51, 52, 53, 55, 56, 57
4	Ward 25, 26, 27, 28, 30	16	Ward 54, 74, 77
5	Ward 13, 20, 24, 31, 50, 106	17	Ward 46, 47, 48, 60
6	Ward 2, 9, 10, 12, 22	18	Ward 63, 65, 66, 68, 80, 110
7	Ward 21, 101, 102, 103, 105	19	Ward 43, 61, 64, 67, 69
8	Ward 83, 84, 85, 86, 100	20	Ward 58, 59, 62, 71, 72, 73
9	Ward 18, 87, 89, 90, 91	21	Ward 11, 14, 17, 19, 108
10	Ward 92, 93, 94, 99	22	Ward 15, 16, 109
11	Ward 42, 44, 45, 49	23	Ward 75, 76, 88
12	Ward 78, 79, 81, 82	24	Ward 95, 96, 97, 98

CONTENT:

WIND ROSES
WEATHER ICONS
PLANTS, TREES & MOUNTAINS
OVERALL
CITY NAMES

LEGENDS

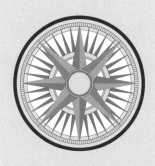

TMDT-163

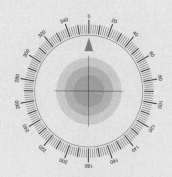

TMDT-164

TMDT-165

TMDT-166

TMDT-167

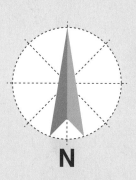

TMDT-168

TMDT-169

TMDT-170

TMDT-171

TMDT-173

TMDT-174

TMDT-175

TMDT-176

TMDT-177

TMDT-178

TMDT-179

TMDT-180

TMDT-181

TMDT-182

TMDT-183

TMDT-184

TMDT-185

TMDT-186

TMDT-187

TMDT-188

TMDT-189

TMDT-190

°F

TMDT-191

°C

TMDT-192

N|A

TMDT-193

TMDT-194

TMDT-195

TMDT-196

TMDT-197

TMDT-198

TMDT-199

TMDT-200

TMDT-201

TMDT-202

TMDT-203

TMDT-204

TMDT-205

TMDT-206

TMDT-207

TMDT-208

TMDT-209

TMDT-210

TMDT-211

TMDT-212

TMDT-213

TMDT-214

TMDT-215

TMDT-216

TMDT-217

TMDT-218

TMDT-219

TMDT-220

TMDT-221

TMDT-222

TMDT-223

TMDT-224

TMDT-225

TMDT-226

TMDT-227

TMDT-228

TMDT-229

TMDT-230

TMDT-231

TMDT-232

TMDT-233

TMDT-234

TMDT-235

TMDT-236

TMDT-237

TMDT-238

TMDT-239

TMDT-240

TMDT-241

TMDT-242

TMDT-243

TMDT-244

TMDT-245

TMDT-246

TMDT-247

TMDT-248

TMDT-249

TMDT-250

TMDT-251

TMDT-252

TMDT-253

TMDT-254

TMDT-255

TMDT-256

TMDT-257

TMDT-258

TMDT-259

TMDT-260

TMDT-261

TMDT-262

TMDT-263

TMDT-264

°City

TMDT-265

CITY

TMDT-266

TMDT-267

CITY

TMDT-268

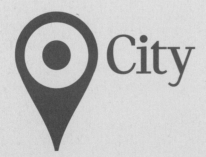City

TMDT-269

CITY

TMDT-270

TMDT-271

CITY

TMDT-272

TMDT-273

CITY

TMDT-274

TMDT-275

City

TMDT-276

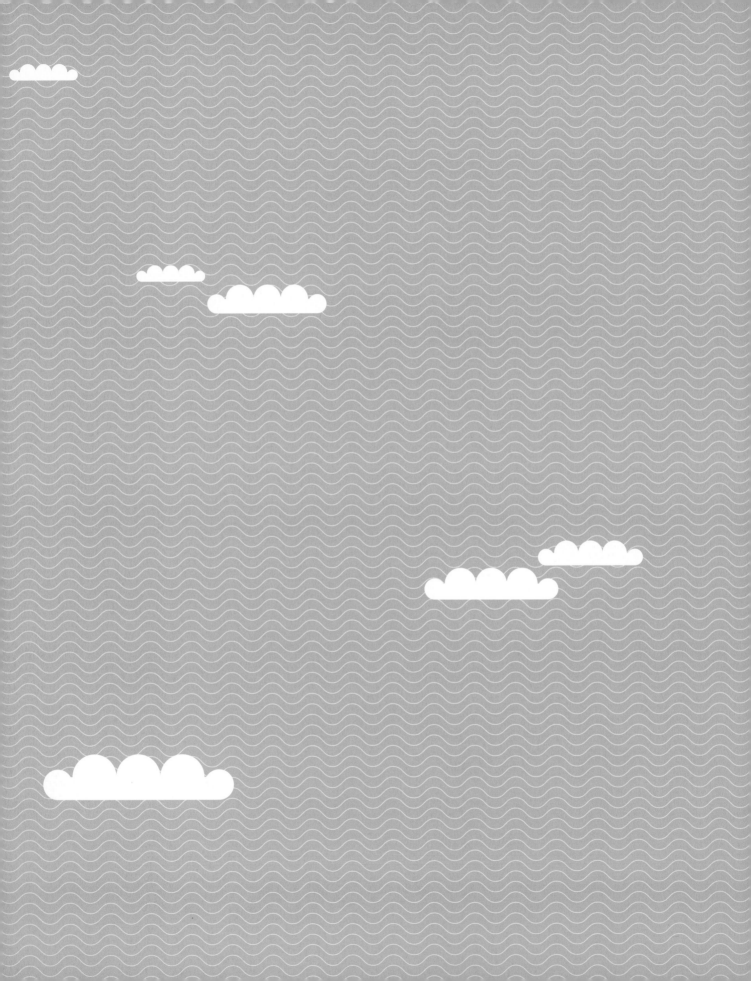

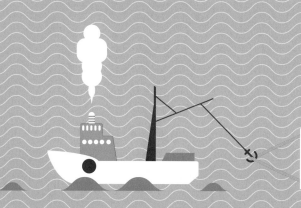

TMDT-277

TMDT-278

TMDT-279

TMDT-280

TMDT-281

TMDT-282

TMDT-283

TMDT-284

TMDT-285

TMDT-286

TMDT-287

TMDT-288

TMDT-289

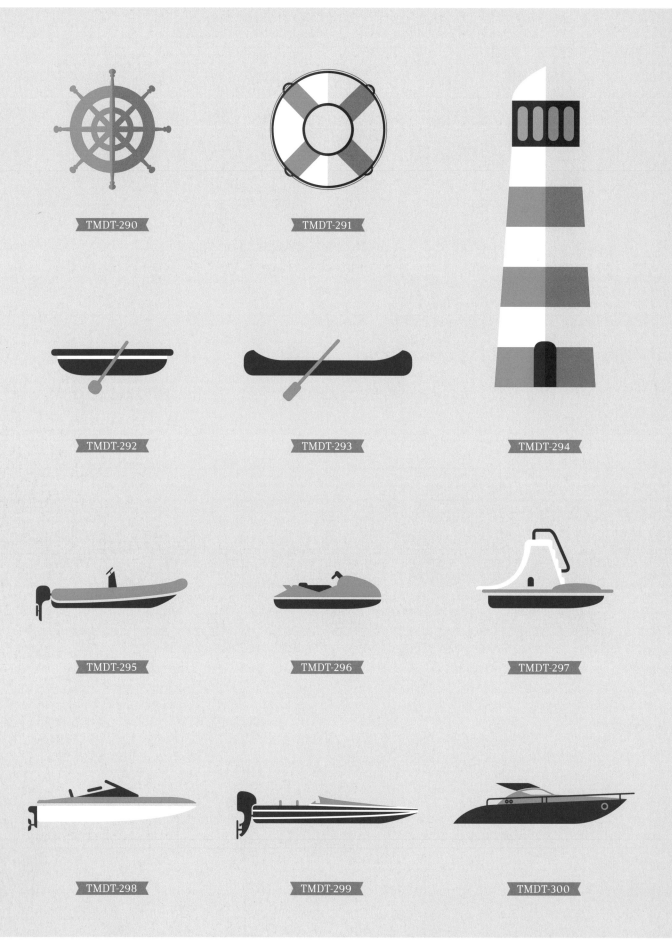

TMDT-290

TMDT-291

TMDT-292

TMDT-293

TMDT-294

TMDT-295

TMDT-296

TMDT-297

TMDT-298

TMDT-299

TMDT-300

TMDT-301

TMDT-302

TMDT-303

TMDT-304

TMDT-305

TMDT-306

TMDT-307

TMDT-308

TMDT-309

TMDT-310

TMDT-311

TMDT-312

TMDT-313

TMDT-314

TMDT-315

TMDT-316

TMDT-317

TMDT-318

TMDT-319

TMDT-320

TMDT-321

TMDT-322

TMDT-323

TMDT-324

TMDT-325

TMDT-326

TMDT-327

TMDT-328

TMDT-329

TMDT-330

TMDT-331

TMDT-332

TMDT-333

TMDT-334

TMDT-335

TMDT-336

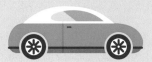

TMDT-337

TMDT-338

TMDT-339

TMDT-340

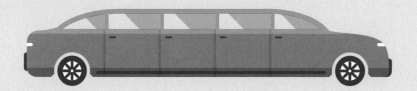

TMDT-341

TMDT-342

TMDT-343

TMDT-344

TMDT-345

TMDT-346

TMDT-347

TMDT-348

TMDT-349

TMDT-350

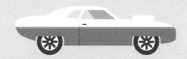

TMDT-351

TMDT-352

TMDT-353

TMDT-354

TMDT-355

TMDT-356

TMDT-357

TMDT-358

TMDT-359

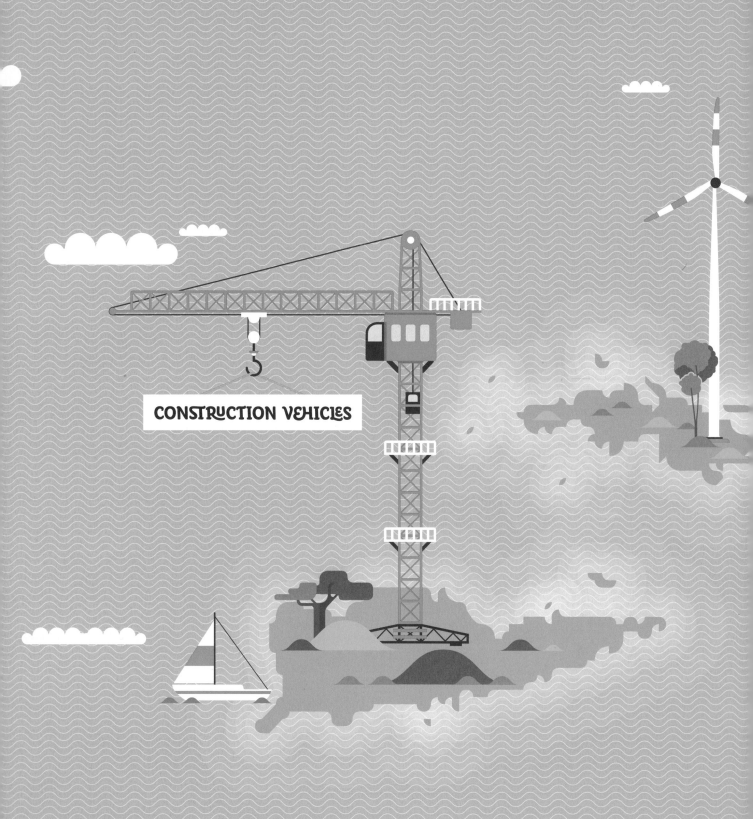

CONSTRUCTION VEHICLES

TMDT-360

TMDT-361

TMDT-362

TMDT-363

TMDT-364

TMDT-365

TMDT-366

TMDT-367

TMDT-368

TMDT-370

TMDT-371

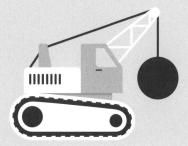

TMDT-372

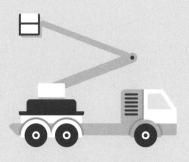

TMDT-373

TMDT-374

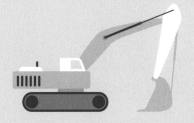

TMDT-375

TMDT-376

TMDT-377

TMDT-378

TMDT-379

TMDT-380

TMDT-381

TMDT-382

TMDT-383

TMDT-384

TMDT-385

TMDT-386

TMDT-387

TMDT-388

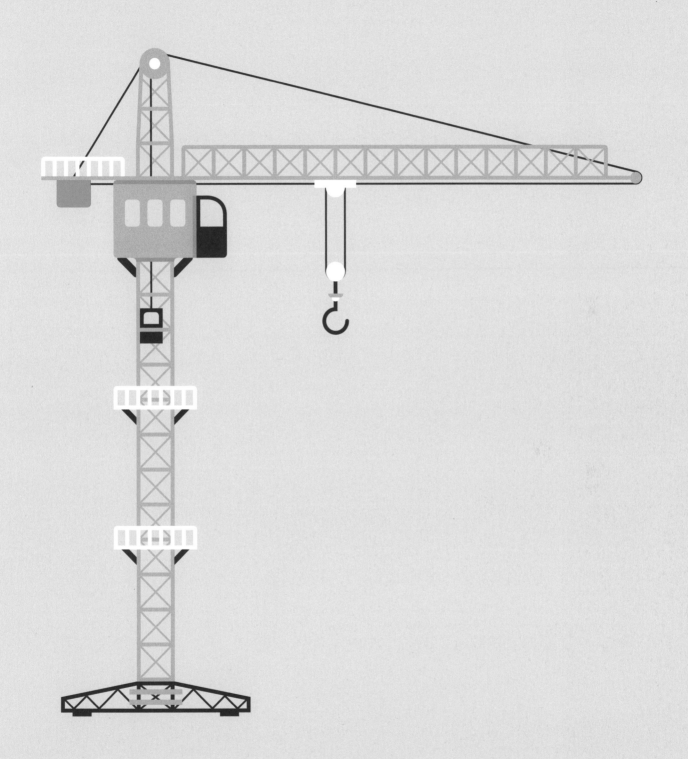

TMDT-389

Strawberry   Blueberry   Candy

Melon   Pistachio   Vanilla

Kiwi   Bubble Gum   Apple

0.99$

TMDT-390

TMDT-391

TMDT-392

TMDT-393

TMDT-394

TMDT-395

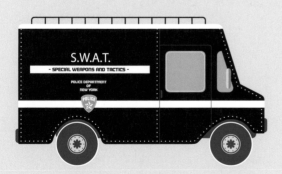

TMDT-396

TMDT-397

TMDT-398

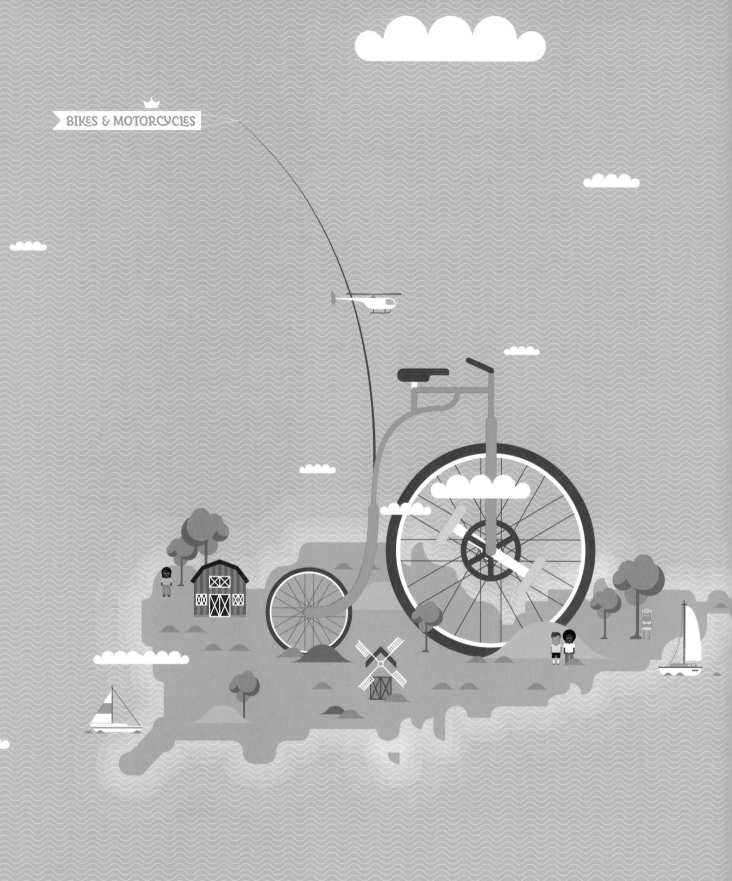

TMDT-399

TMDT-400

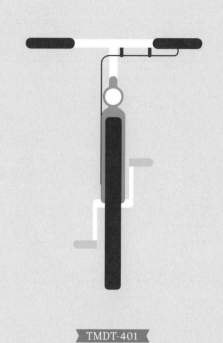

TMDT-401

TMDT-402

TMDT-403

TMDT-404

TMDT-405

TMDT-406

TMDT-407

TMDT-408

TMDT-409

TMDT-410

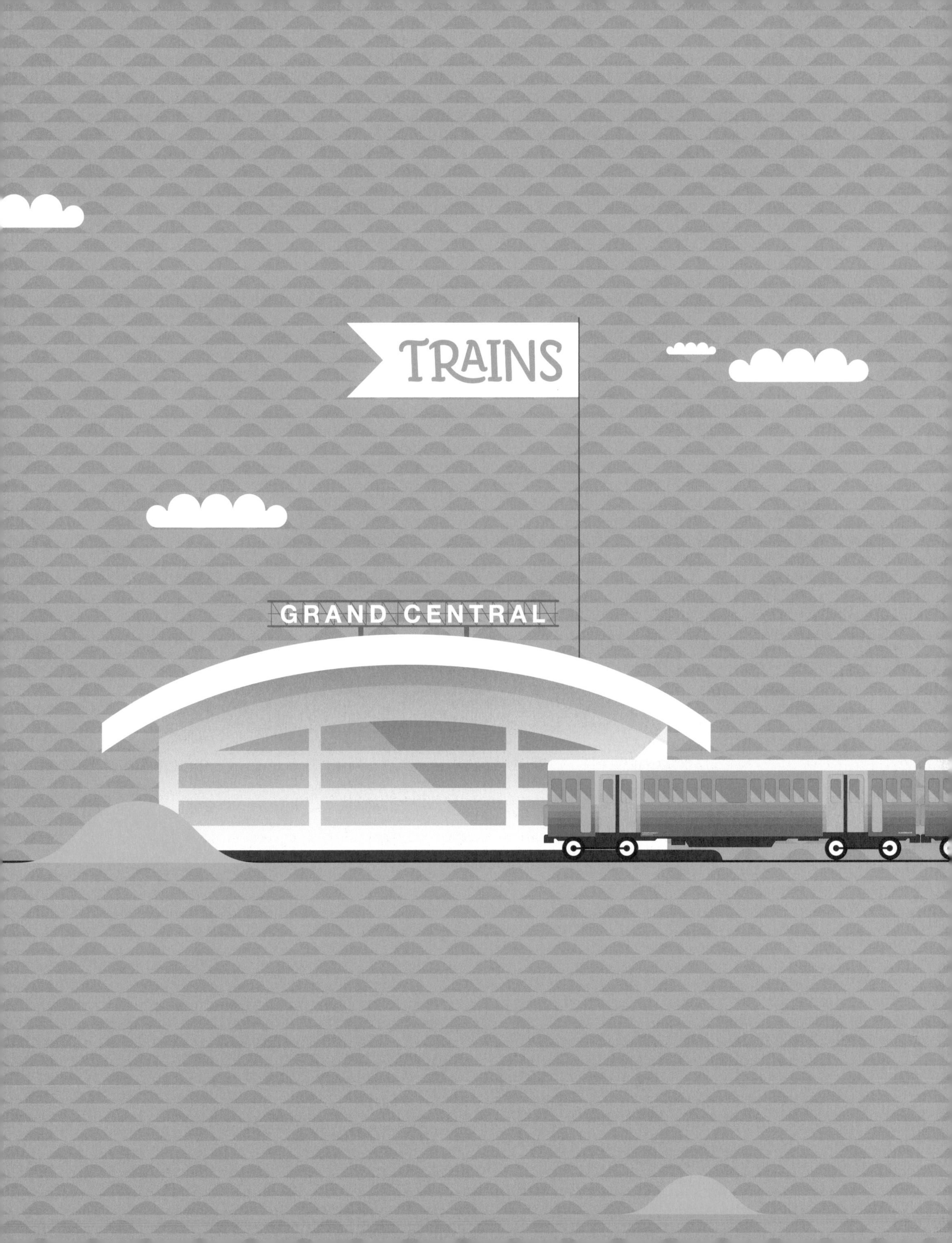
TRAINS
GRAND CENTRAL

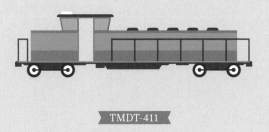

TMDT-411

TMDT-412

TMDT-413

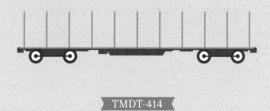

TMDT-414

TMDT-415

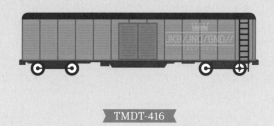

TMDT-416

TMDT-417

TMDT-418

TMDT-419

TMDT-420

TMDT-421

TMDT-422

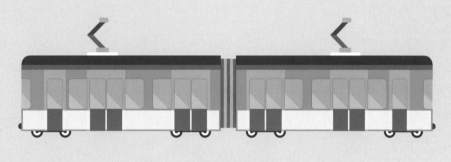

TMDT-423

TMDT-424

TMDT-425

TMDT-426

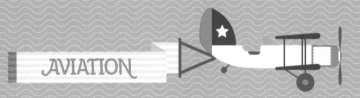

AIRPORT

TMDT-427

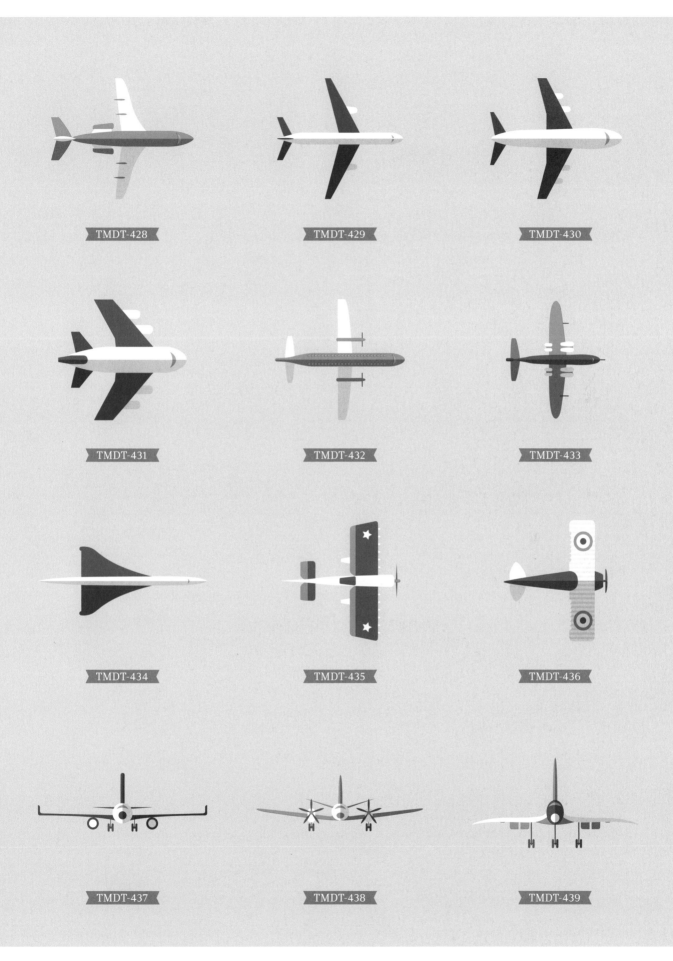

TMDT-428

TMDT-429

TMDT-430

TMDT-431

TMDT-432

TMDT-433

TMDT-434

TMDT-435

TMDT-436

TMDT-437

TMDT-438

TMDT-439

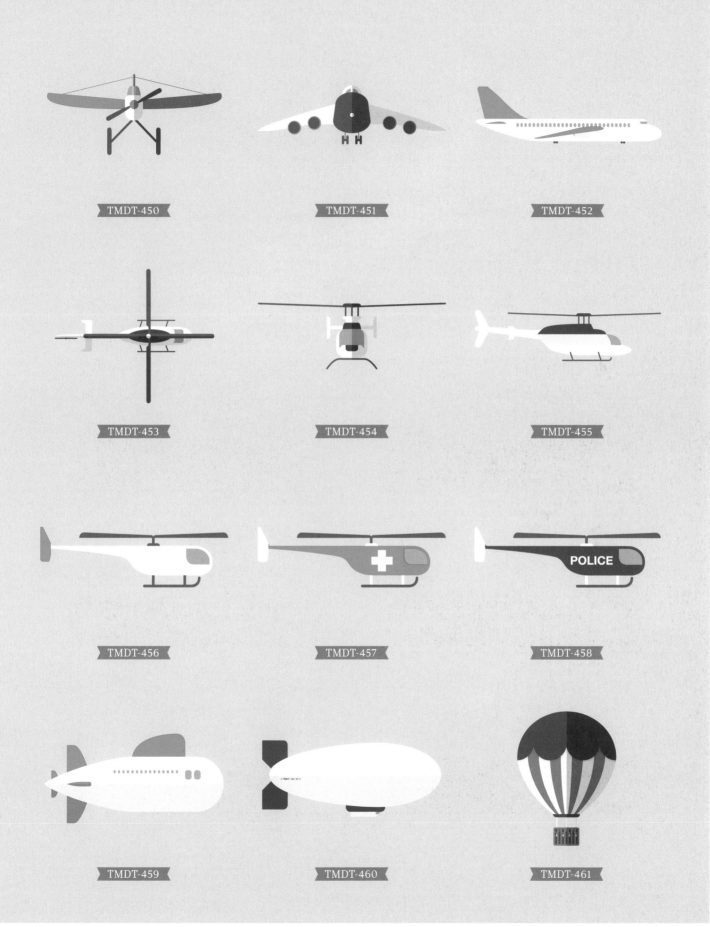

TMDT-450

TMDT-451

TMDT-452

TMDT-453

TMDT-454

TMDT-455

TMDT-456

TMDT-457

TMDT-458

TMDT-459

TMDT-460

TMDT-461

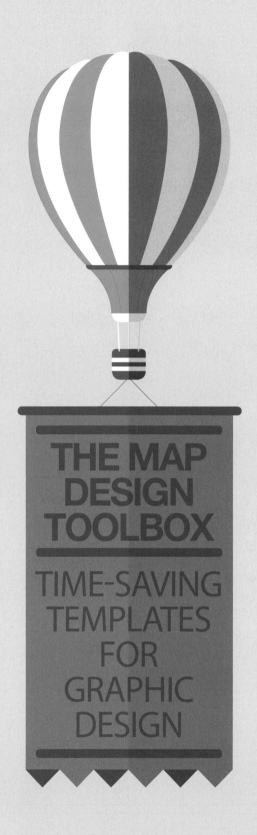

THE MAP DESIGN TOOLBOX

TIME-SAVING TEMPLATES FOR GRAPHIC DESIGN

TMDT-462

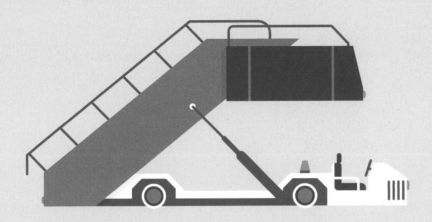

TMDT-463

TMDT-464

TMDT-465

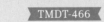

TMDT-466

TMDT-467

TMDT-468

TMDT-469

TMDT-470

BUILDINGS

TMDT-471

TMDT-472

TMDT-473

TMDT-474

TMDT-475

TMDT-476

TMDT-477

TMDT-478

TMDT-479

TMDT-480

TMDT-481

TMDT-482

TMDT-483

TMDT-484

TMDT-485

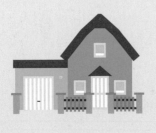

TMDT-486

TMDT-487

TMDT-488

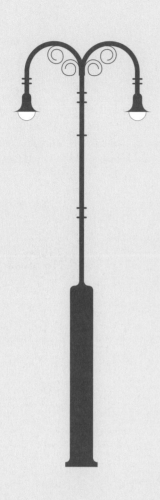

TMDT-490

TMDT-491

TMDT-489

TMDT-492

TMDT-493

TMDT-494

TMDT-495

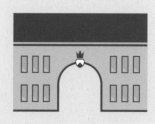

TMDT-496

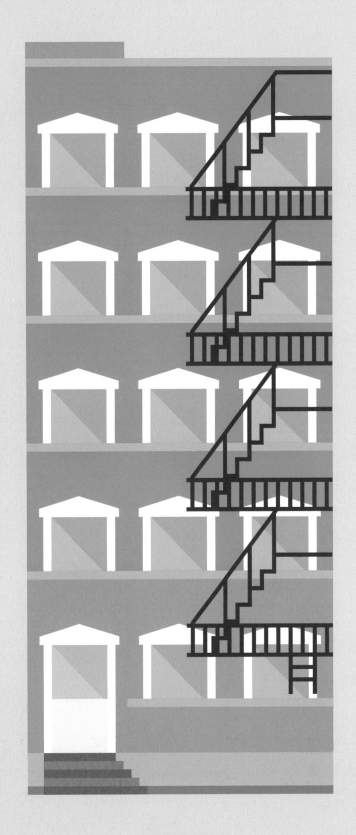

TMDT-497

TMDT-498

TMDT-499

TMDT-500

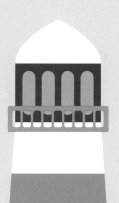

TMDT-501

TMDT-502

TMDT-503

TMDT-504

TMDT-505

TMDT-507

TMDT-508

TMDT-509

TMDT-510

TMDT-511

TMDT-512

TMDT-513

TMDT-514

TMDT-515

TMDT-516

TMDT-518

TMDT-519

TMDT-517

TMDT-520

TMDT-521

TMDT-522

TMDT-523

TMDT-524

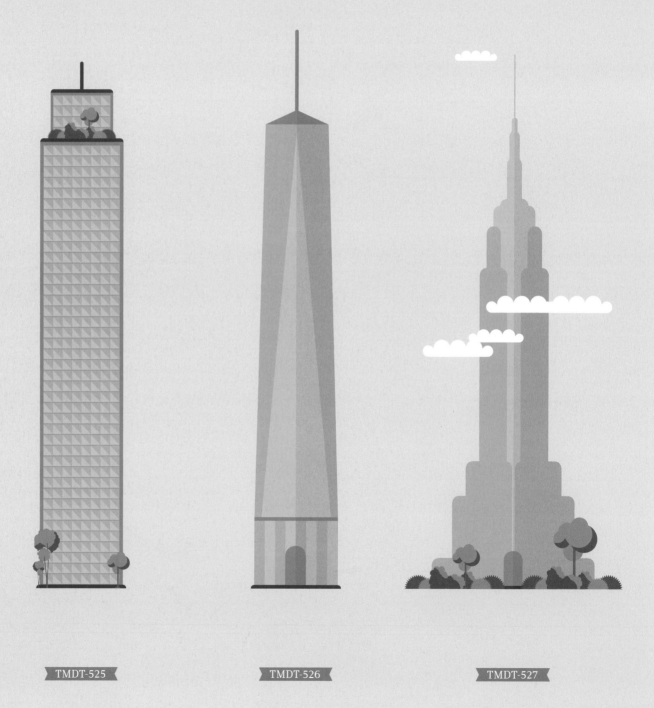

TMDT-525

TMDT-526

TMDT-527

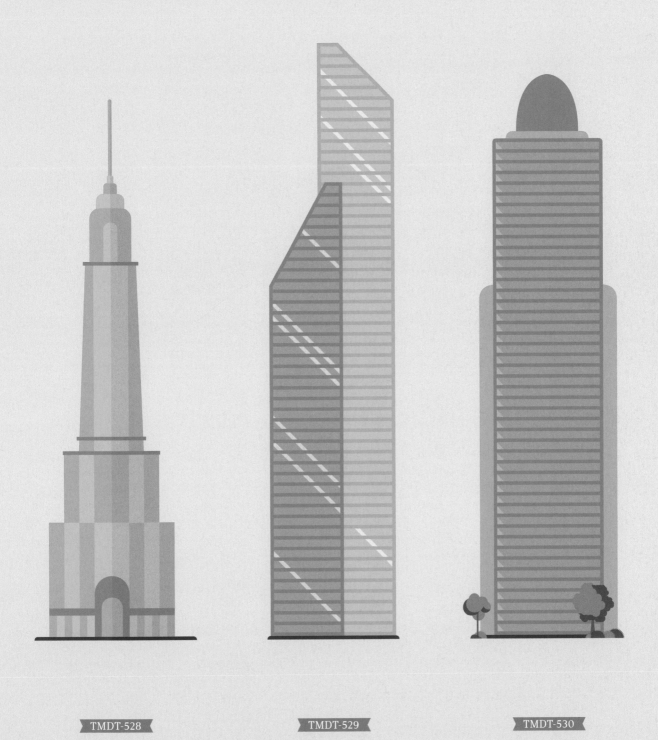

TMDT-528

TMDT-529

TMDT-530

TMDT-531

TMDT-532

TMDT-533

TMDT-534

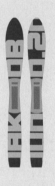

TMDT-535

TMDT-536

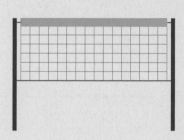

TMDT-537

TMDT-538

TMDT-539

TMDT-540

194

TMDT-541

TMDT-542

TMDT-543

TMDT-544

TMDT-545

TMDT-546

TMDT-547

TMDT-548

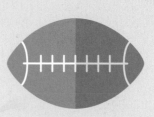

TMDT-549

JAKOB
THE
MIGHTY
SK8
BOARDER

TMDT-550

TMDT-551

TMDT-552

TMDT-553

TMDT-554

TMDT-555

TMDT-556

TMDT-557

TMDT-558

TMDT-559

#23
THE GREATEST
OF ALL TIMES.

TMDT-560

TMDT-561

TMDT-562

TMDT-563

TMDT-564

TMDT-565

TMDT-566

TMDT-567

TMDT-568

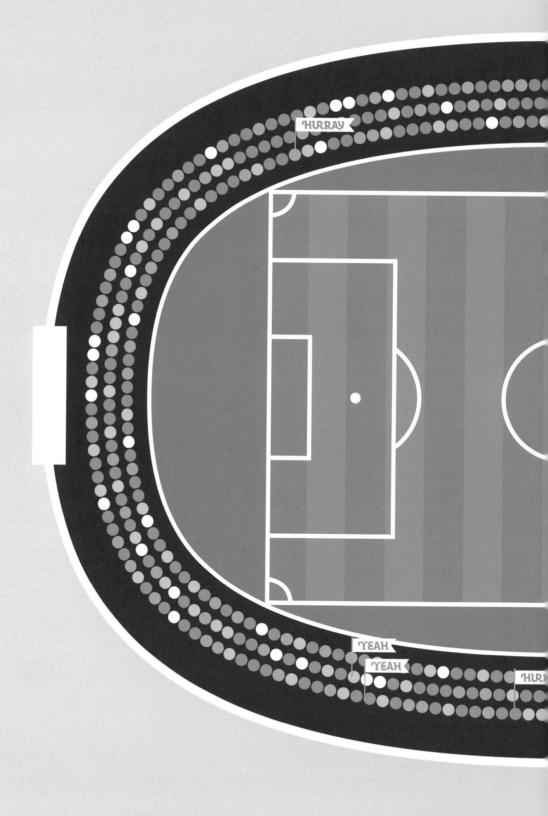

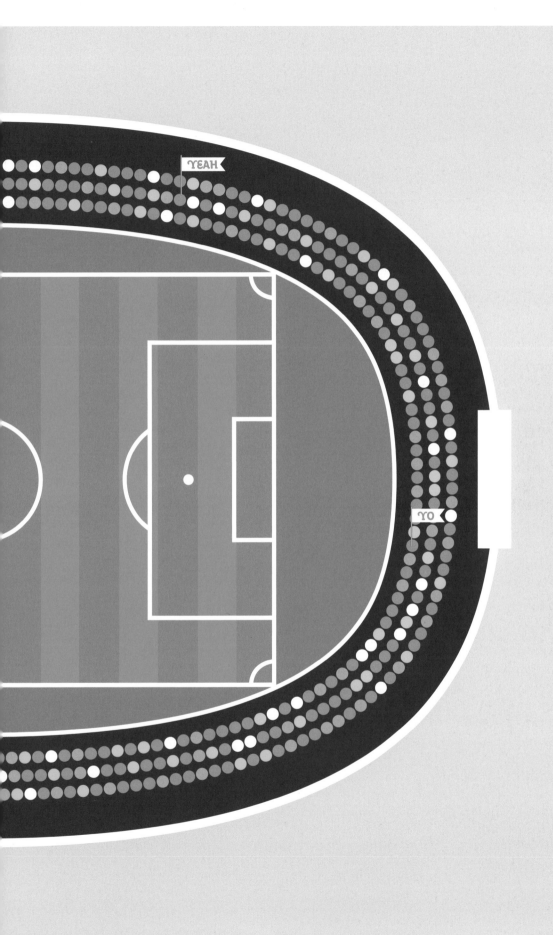

YUMMY ICE CREAM

TSCHEBU & SON
ICE CREAM

TMDT-570

TMDT-571

TMDT-572

TMDT-573

TMDT-574

TMDT-575

TMDT-576

TMDT-577

TMDT-578

TMDT-579

TMDT-580

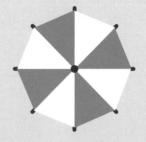

TMDT-581

TMDT-582

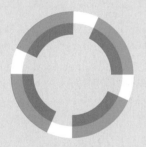

TMDT-583

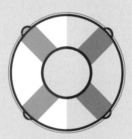

TMDT-584

TMDT-585

TMDT-586

TMDT-587

TMDT-588

TMDT-589

TMDT-590

TMDT-591

TMDT-592

TMDT-593

TMDT-594

TMDT-595

TMDT-596

TMDT-597

TMDT-598

TMDT-599

TMDT-600

TMDT-601

TMDT-602

TMDT-603

TMDT-604

TMDT-605

TMDT-606

TMDT-607

TMDT-608

TMDT-609

TMDT-610

TMDT-611

TMDT-612

TMDT-613

TMDT-614

TMDT-615

211

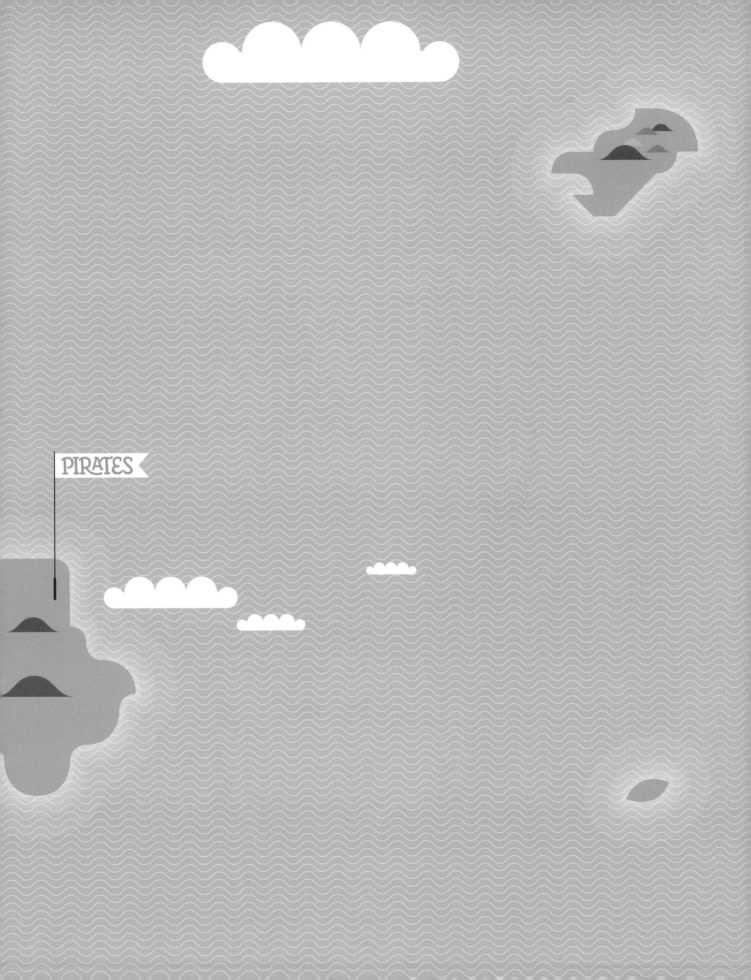

PIRATES

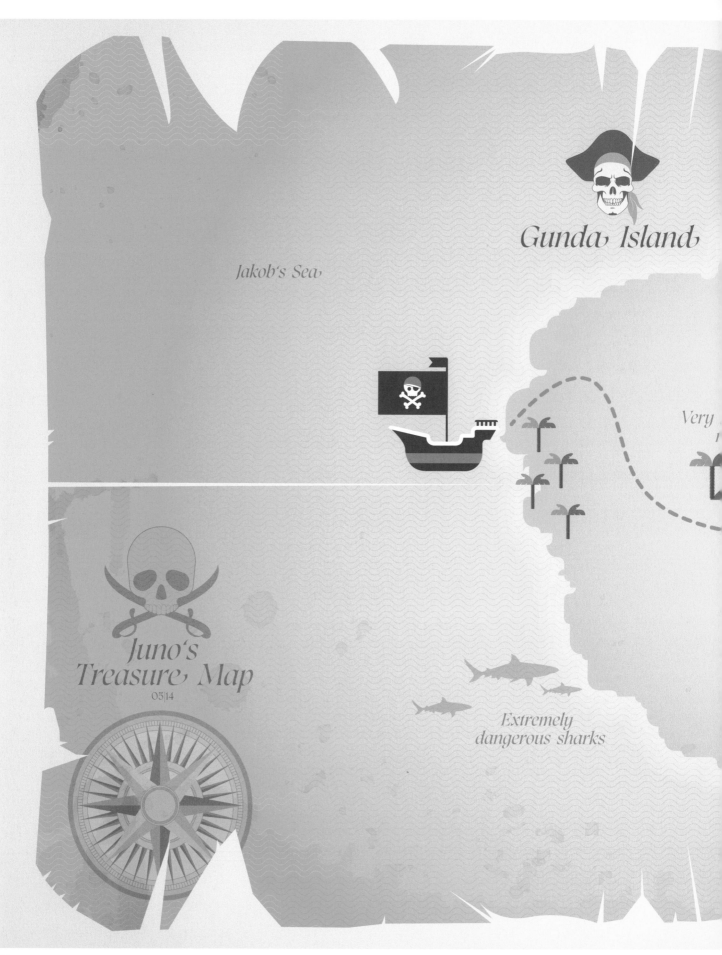

Gunda Island

Jakob's Sea

Very

Juno's
Treasure Map
05|4

Extremely
dangerous sharks

Really
high tree

Treasure

ain

Jakob's Sea

TMDT-616

215

TMDT-617

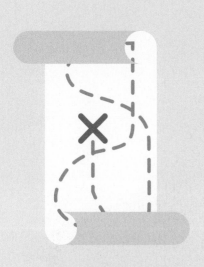

TMDT-619

TMDT-620

TMDT-618

TMDT-621

TMDT-622

TMDT-623

TMDT-624

TMDT-625

TMDT-626

TMDT-627

TMDT-628

TMDT-629

TMDT-630

TMDT-631

TMDT-632

TMDT-633

TMDT-634

TMDT-635

TMDT-636

TMDT-637

TMDT-638

TMDT-639

TMDT-640

TMDT-641

TMDT-642

TMDT-643

TMDT-644

TMDT-645

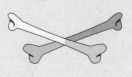

TMDT-646

TMDT-647

TMDT-648

TMDT-649

The

End

GUNDA
I LOVE YOU!

MY WONDERFUL KIDS
JUNO
JAKOB

IMPRINT

The Map Design Toolbox
Time-Saving Templates for Graphic Design

By Alexander Tibelius

Cover and layout by Alexander Tibelius
Texts by Noelia Hobeika

Typefaces:
Berg by Andreas Søren Johansen,
Caligo by Aron Jancso,
Canary by Mark Frömberg,
Fonster by Kathrin Esser,
High Times by Tilo Pentzin,
Mevum by Angelo Stitz,
Regular by Nik Thoenen,
Relevant by Mika Mischler and Nik Thoenen,
Foundry: www.gestaltenfonts.com

Proofreading by Felix Lennert
Printed by Nino Druck GmbH, Neustadt/Weinstraße

Made in Germany

Published by Gestalten, Berlin 2014
ISBN 978-3-89955-541-7

A DVD is included in the book.

Respect copyrights, encourage creativity!

For more information, please visit www.gestalten.com.

Bibliographic information published by
the Deutsche Nationalbibliothek.
The Deutsche Nationalbibliothek lists this
publication in the Deutsche Nationalbibliografie;
detailed bibliographic data are available
online at http://dnb.d-nb.de.

This book was printed on paper certified
according to the standards of the FSC®.

Gestalten is a climate-neutral company. We
collaborate with the non-profit carbon offset provider
myclimate (www.myclimate.org) to neutralize the
company's carbon footprint produced through our
worldwide business activities by investing in projects that
reduce CO_2 emissions (www.gestalten.com/myclimate).